はじめに

　ラダーシリーズは、「はしご (ladder)」を使って一歩一歩上を目指すように、学習者の実力に合わせ、無理なくステップアップできるよう開発された英文リーダーのシリーズです。

　リーディング力をつけるためには、繰り返したくさん読むこと、いわゆる「多読」がもっとも効果的な学習法であると言われています。多読では、「1.速く　2.訳さず英語のまま　3.なるべく辞書を使わず」に読むことが大切です。スピードを計るなど、速く読むよう心がけましょう（たとえば TOEIC® テストの音声スピードはおよそ1分間に150語です）。そして1語ずつ訳すのではなく、英語を英語のまま理解するくせをつけるようにします。こうして読み続けるうちに語感がついてきて、だんだんと英語が理解できるようになるのです。まずは、ラダーシリーズの中からあなたのレベルに合った本を選び、少しずつ英文に慣れ親しんでください。たくさんの本を手にとるうちに、英文書がすらすら読めるようになってくるはずです。

《本シリーズの特徴》

- 中学校レベルから中級者レベルまで5段階に分かれています。自分に合ったレベルからスタートしてください。
- クラシックから現代文学、ノンフィクション、ビジネスと幅広いジャンルを扱っています。あなたの興味に合わせてタイトルを選べます。
- 巻末のワードリストで、いつでもどこでも単語の意味を確認できます。レベル1、2では、文中の全ての単語が、レベル3以上は中学校レベル外の単語が掲載されています。
- カバーにヘッドホーンマークのついているタイトルは、オーディオ・サポートがあります。ウェブから購入／ダウンロードし、リスニング教材としても併用できます。

《使用語彙について》

レベル1：中学校で学習する単語約1000語

レベル2：レベル1の単語＋使用頻度の高い単語約300語

レベル3：レベル1の単語＋使用頻度の高い単語約600語

レベル4：レベル1の単語＋使用頻度の高い単語約1000語

レベル5：語彙制限なし

CONTENTS

Prologue..2

The First Story..7
The Second Story....................................15
The Third Story..23
The Fourth Story....................................31
The Fifth Story..51
The Sixth Story..67
The Seventh Story..................................79
The Last Story..87

Word List..92

【年表】

1828年 1月23日　薩摩国鹿児島城下の下級藩士の家に生まれる

1853年 7月　浦賀にペリー来航

1854年 3月　日米和親条約締結

　　　 4月　島津斉彬の近習となり、国事に関わる仕事に携わるようになる

1858年 7月　井伊直弼による安政の大獄が始まる

　　　 9月　月照とともに入水するも一命を取りとめる

　　　12月　幕府の目から逃れるために奄美大島へ島流しとなる

1862年 1月　島津久光の召還状をうけて鹿児島へ戻る

　　　 6月　島津久光の不興を買い、再び島流し、牢に入れられる

1863年 7月　薩英戦争が起こる

1864年 2月　赦免召還され、鹿児島に戻る

　　　 7月　蛤御門の変を起こした長州が第一次長州征伐を受ける

1865年 1月　糸子と結婚

　　　 5月　第二次長州征伐

1866年 1月　薩長同盟締結

1867年10月14日　徳川慶喜、大政奉還を発表、薩長に倒幕の密勅

1868年 1月　鳥羽・伏見の戦い、王政復古の大号令

　　　 3月　勝海舟と江戸城明け渡しの交渉をする

　　　 4月11日　江戸城開城、これ以後、戊辰戦争で各地を転戦することと
　　　　　　　　鹿児島に戻ることを繰り返す

1871年 7月　再三に出仕を促され、新政府の参議に就任

1873年 6月　対朝鮮問題をめぐる新政府首脳の軋轢が表面化

　　　 9月　参議を辞職し下野、鹿児島に戻る

1874年 6月　鹿児島に、陸軍士官要請のための私学校を設立され、大きな勢力
　　　　　　となる

1877年 2月　西南戦争が起こる

　　　 9月24日　城山決戦にて死去

1878年 5月14日　大久保利通が不平士族に暗殺される

1889年　　　西郷隆盛への名誉回復が認められる

1898年12月　西郷隆盛の銅像が上野に完成

Amami-Ōshima
奄美大島

Okino-Edabu
沖永良部島

Ryūkyū Kingdom or Okinawa
琉球王国／沖縄

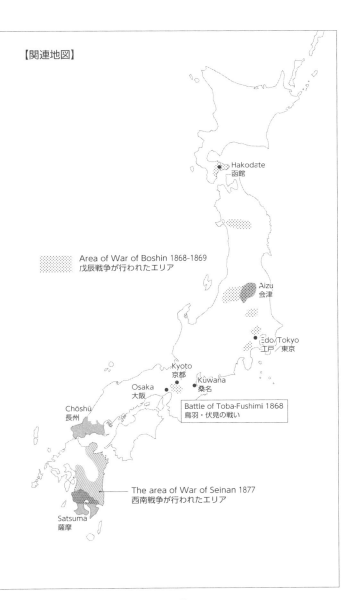

主な登場人物

奄美渡島

Aikana
愛加那
(1837–1902)
安政の大獄で流罪となった隆盛の島妻。

Saigō Takamori
西郷隆盛 (1828–1877)

明治維新の中心人物。参議として新政府に入るが対立し西南戦争の指導者となる。

息子

Satsuma-han 薩摩藩

Saigō Itoko
西郷糸子(1843–1922)
薩摩藩士の娘。西郷の三人目の妻。

Saigō Kikujirō
西郷菊次郎
(1861–1928)
隆盛と島妻・愛加那との間の子ども。糸子に養育される。

薩長同盟 →

Saigō Tsugumichi
西郷従道(1843–1902)
西郷隆盛の弟。西南戦争では政府側についた。

Chōshū-han 長州藩

Yoshida Shōin
吉田松陰(1830–1859)
松下村塾塾長。尊王論者。明治維新の火付け役。

Shimazu Nariakira
島津斉彬(1809–1858)
第11代藩主。西郷や大久保などの人材を見出し育てた。

Shimazu Hisamitsu
島津久光(1817–1887)
薩摩藩の事実上のトップとして明治維新で大きな役割を果たした。

Kido Kōin
木戸孝允(1833–1877)
松下村塾出身。明治維新の中心人物。

Ōkubo Toshimichi
大久保利通(1830–1878)
倒幕・明治維新の中心人物。維新後、西郷と対立し失脚させる。

Itō Hirobumi
伊藤博文(1841–1909)
松下村塾出身。木戸の元従者、新政府で活躍し元老となる。

Ōyama Iwao
大山巌(1842–1916)
西郷隆盛の従兄弟。西南戦争を始め数々の戦争を指揮した。

Bakufu 幕府

Tokugawa Iesada
徳川家定 (1824-1858)
第13代将軍。幼少より病弱で黒船来航後ほどなく死去。

養子縁組

Atsuko / Tenshō-In
篤子／天璋院 (1836-1883)
島津家の一族の生まれ。大政奉還後、徳川家と新政府の調停に尽力した。

Tokugawa Iemochi
徳川家茂 (1846-1866)
第14代将軍。20歳の若さで死去。

Kazuno-miya
和宮親子内親王 (1846-1877)
京都生まれの皇女。降嫁して将軍徳川家茂の正室となる。

Tokugawa Yoshinobu
徳川慶喜 (1837-1913)
江戸幕府最後の将軍。新政権にも関わりを持ち、生涯を全うした。

Ii Naosuke
井伊直弼 (1815-1860)
江戸幕府の大老。攘夷派の浪士たちに桜田門外で暗殺された。

Katsu Kaishū
勝海舟 (1823-1899)
幕府の軍艦奉行。維新後、新政府でも旧幕臣の代表者として重きを置かれた。

Saitō Hajime
斉藤一 (1844-1915)
新撰組幹部。維新後は警視庁に採用され、警視隊に所属して西南戦争に従軍。

Kuwana-han 桑名藩

Tatsumi Naobumi
立見尚文 (1845-1907)
旧幕府軍出身者ながら、新政府でも能力を買われて陸軍で活躍する。

Imperial Court 朝廷

Emperor Kōmei
孝明天皇 (1831-1867)
第121代天皇。保守派の攘夷主義者。

異母妹

Emperor Meiji
明治天皇 (1852-1912)
第122代天皇。徳川慶喜から政権奉還を受ける。

Saigō Takamori
Coen Nishiumi

Prologue

It was uncomfortable inside the cave on Shiroyama mountain. Saigō Takamori and his men had walked miles and miles in these mountains trying to get back home. But the enemy was out there, and the enemy controlled the terrain.

They had been camped in this humid cave for five days now. Watching the flame of a candle, Saigō remembered his time in the prison cell on Okino-Erabu island, far to the south of Kagoshima, Satsuma's capital on the southern tip of Kyushu. Now his days were drawing to an end. Saigō recalled countless things from his past, including his life as a prisoner on that tiny island.

"When I was in that cell, I was so exhausted I couldn't stand. I was just like an insect," Saigō said and laughed. Kirino, his long-time general, listened with a quiet smile.

Saigō and his men had ignored the urgings

of the enemy to surrender. Several times they warned him. But Saigō would always reply, "I have fought against the emperor's army. I must take responsibility." How skilled and professional the Imperial Army had become, he thought. Indeed, for it was Saigō who had systematically organized and trained them.

He thought of the Emperor Meiji when he was just a boy. Saigō taught *sumo* wrestling at the imperial court, and didn't hesitate to throw him to the ground because he needed this new emperor to be a tough ruler. At such an important moment in Japanese history, the emperor had to be strong. Recent emperors, however, had not been expected or required to be leaders of warriors and had been raised by ladies of the court. It was Saigō who had changed this tradition. And the young Emperor Meiji had liked him and responded well to his training.

It was just before dawn on September 24, 1877. This was the day government forces warned they would launch their attack. The government army already had Saigō's soldiers surrounded. Everybody knew that this would be the last battle after seven months of brutal warfare.

After thanking one and all, Saigō Takamori ordered his soldiers to march toward the enemy. There was an autumn morning mist. And the sound of crickets. Suddenly gunfire exploded from the enemy line. Saigō and his soldiers marched toward the bullets. How long they walked nobody knows. Then, in an instant, bullets slammed into Saigō's leg and shoulder.

When he felt the keen pain, Saigō understood: everything was over. "Fine. This is it. I am ready. Ah, it seems this is my time to go." Saigō was calm. He had prepared fully for this moment.

Saigō sat in formal posture on the ground and bowed deeply toward the east, in the direction of Tokyo, in the direction of the palace of Emperor Meiji. Now, Saigō shut his eyes. His men immediately knew what to do.

"Sir, forgive me," Beppu, one of his followers, cried. And he lopped Saigō's neck off with his sword.

PROLOGUE

Saigō Takamori was forty-nine years old.

Everybody sobbed. Beppu with both hands took up Saigō's head, and he then wrapped it in a cloth.

The enemy was approaching. Beppu quickly buried Saigō's body in the ground. Then he killed himself. He was thirty-nine years old.

The others bowed deeply toward the site where Saigō lay. And then, they launched one last attack against the government troops.

The battle was finished around 9 a.m. Saigō's defeat marked the end of the last civil war in Japanese history. This War of Seinan—so-called because the battlefields were spread across the seinan or southwestern area of Japan—cost countless lives and brought old friends and partners into a series of painful engagements.

Saigō Takamori had been the former first minister of the reformed Japanese modern army. So he and his generals had in fact been fighting against their old colleagues. This is the story of the long path that led to Saigō's final battle. It is a story of success, struggle, and accomplishment, and of the final disappointment and despair of one of the most famous heroes of Japan's modern history.

The last Headquarters of Saigō's army. Called "Saigō Cave"
by Doricono / Wikipedia

The First Story

My name is Saitō Hajime. I am a former samurai working for the Shinsen-gumi in Kyoto. The Shinsen-gumi is the special police force serving the Tokugawa government. It was formed in 1863.

Let me give you some background. U.S. steam-powered battleships arrived on our shores in the 1850s and demanded that Japan open its ports to the Western world. Everybody called these Western ships "Black Ships" because their hulls were covered in dark pitch.

Japan did not have any big and modern steamships like the Black Ships. Our technology had basically stayed the same for over two hundred years because foreign trading and contact with westeners was strictly prohibited.

After encountering the fleet of Black Ships, the government—the Tokugawa shogunate—rescinded its policy of seclusion and reluctantly started trading with the West. The Japanese leaders entered into an unfair trading treaty because they had little knowledge of international affairs. After the U.S., the British, French, Dutch, and Russians came, too, and the shogunate made the same bad deals with them.

Many educated samurai felt gravely threatened when faced with the Western global powers and their advanced technologies. And everyone was furious at the shogun's pathetic and shameful reaction in response to them.

Many people thus came to believe that Japan must be reformed. They thought that, in order to resist Western pressure, Japan should be unified under the imperial court instead of being ruled by a shogun. Japan would fight back against the barbarian invaders with the spirit of the samurai.

From the foreigners' point of view, the Japanese political system was quite complicated. For hundreds of years, emperors who were considered all-powerful and divine had granted all temporal powers—executive, judicial, and legislative—to a shogun, who was basically a warrior-class dictator.

Under the authority of the shogun's strong hegemony, over three hundred local lords served the central government. But each lord had his own *han*—fief or domain—that he governed as if it were a sovereign nation.

Now, after encountering the Westerners with their advanced technology, our country found itself divided between the pro-emperor faction and the pro-shogun loyalists.

Some brave people did try to fight the foreign powers. But they were easily defeated. I am amazed that my country was able to survive without being invaded by the Western nations. Elsewhere in Asia, many other nations were forced to relinquish their independence. Even China was infringed upon and divided up by Western powers.

Since our emperor was located in Kyoto, many activists who wanted to support the imperial court went there. Well, for me, as a poor samurai, or warrior, this provided a great opportunity to work for the shogun's government, which was desperate to retain control.

In the feudal era, it would have been almost

impossible for a person like me, who came from the lower ranks, to be promoted. But this was not a normal time. The government recruited me and others like me to join a special police force called the Shinsen-gumi, and it was our job to suppress the rebellious samurai in Kyoto.

It was the summer of 1864 when I saw Saigō Takamori for the first time. It was in Kyoto. In those days, we were on the lookout for radical samurai who were trying to manipulate the imperial court. They wanted the emperor to order the shogun to drive the Westerners out of our country. Many of these rebels came from Chōshū, a powerful domain in western Japan dominated by pro-emperor samurai.

Another powerful domain, Aizu, was located in northern Japan. The lord of Aizu was known as a pro-shogun leader. The lord of Aizu decided to set up operations in Kyoto in an attempt to keep control of the court under the authority of the shogun. It was he who formed the Shinsen-gumi that I was working for.

I must now say something about Satsuma. Satsuma, located on the southern end of

Kyushu, was another influential domain in the shogun's government. Satsuma was trying to work with Aizu to achieve harmony between the shogun's government and the imperial court. Saigō was employed by the lord of Satsuma and was one of the key figures coordinating this effort in Kyoto.

Despite these efforts, the activists from Chōshū and other domains were quite persistent. Therefore we, the samurai of Shinsengumi, were kept busy watching their every movement. In July of 1864, we raided their secret meeting place, the Ikedaya Inn, in downtown Kyoto. We killed and arrested many activists mainly linked with Chōshū.

Finally, a battle between Satsuma-Aizu and Chōshū broke out on August 20, 1864. During the series of fights around the Imperial Palace I saw Saigō commanding his men.

He was tall and husky. His big eyes were impressive. His penetrating stare made it impossible for anyone to lie to or attempt to deceive him.

The battles lasted from August 20 to 22, and

THE FIRST STORY

we finally swept Chōshū and its sympathizers from Kyoto.

However, after that battle, I became suspicious about Saigō. And I secretly kept track of his behavior, because it seemed that he was wavering on whether or not it was good for Japan to keep the shogun in power.

Saigō had originally been a pro-emperor samurai. I knew this because he was a friend of Gesshō, a fanatic anti-Westerner and pro-emperor activist who died in 1858.

The Second Story

My name is Atsuko. I am the wife of the thirteenth shogun. His name is Tokugawa Iesada.

Since 1603, the position of shogun had been held by a succession of members of the Tokugawa family. It was when my husband was in power that Commodore Perry came to Japan with his fleet and demanded we open trading relations with the U.S.

I remember that, with the arrival of the U.S. fleet, Japan fell into a period of chaos. Had Japan not been targeted by Western nations like the U.S., no one would have ever heard of Saigō Takamori. Nor would the era of Tokugawa rule have come to an end.

I know Saigō very well because I came from Satsuma, too. It was the idea of Shimazu Nariakira, the lord of Satsuma, to promote Saigō from his low samurai rank. Obeying Nariakira's directive, Saigō developed a strong network among the aristocrats in Kyoto. And as a result, the lord Nariakira adopted a daughter belonging to one of his high-rank samurai clans and then arranged for her marriage with the thirteenth shogun in 1856. That daughter was me.

Saigō Takamori was born on January 23, 1828. He was eight years older than I. Around that time, like many other domains in Japan, Satsuma had serious financial problems. And so did Saigō's family. Saigō was so poor that he could not even keep a wife.

However, I remember that Saigō was exceedingly bright. The lord Shimazu Nariakira recognized his talent. During the lord's time in power, Satsuma's economy revived thanks to the sugar trade. Sugar was produced in Satsuma's southern islands. Satsuma also had quite a strong presence in the Ryūkyū Kingdom farther to the south, through which the province expanded its trading business farther overseas.

As the result of such successes, Satsuma became one of the most influential domains within the Tokugawa government. Unfortunately, Nariakira died in 1858. That same year

Iesada, my husband, died. Our marriage had lasted less than two years. Iesada's health was always poor. He was a lonely shogun who was uncomfortable with others. And, after his decline and death, the power of the Tokugawa grew weaker and weaker. As Iesada's widow, I took the name Tenshō-In.

Before my marriage, I had met Saigō many times. Saigō was a truly loyal man. He served his lord sincerely. So when Nariakira passed away, Saigō was deeply saddened. The year 1858 was a terrible year. I lost my husband. I lost my strongest supporter, the lord of Satsuma. And I was about to lose Saigō, too.

It is unfortunate that Nariakira's successor did not like Saigō. After Nariakira's and my husband's deaths, Satsuma ended up on the wrong side of the political wrangling over the next shogun's succession. Consequently, Satsuma's influence on the Tokugawa clan diminished. The new Tokugawa shogunate led by chief minister Ii Naosuke tried to suppress all political pro-emperor sentiment and activities. Ii hated the fact that many of the pro-emperor intellectuals wanted to kick the Westerners out of our nation.

Remember, it was my husband who had decided to open trade to the U.S. So basically, Ii was in favor of the policy that my husband had developed. However, he despised Satsuma and its ambitions to gain power in the Tokugawa shogunate. I felt sad that Ii turned against Satsuma because of its support of Tokugawa Yoshinobu as successor. In the end, it was Tokugawa Iemochi who became the fourteenth shogun. But he died young in the middle of the war against the Chōshū domain. Then Yoshinobu became the fifteenth shogun in 1866.

Under Ii's directives, many activists were prosecuted. Among them was a monk named Gesshō. He was Saigō's friend whom Saigō tried to hide. Eventually Saigō went back to Satsuma with Gesshō. But since Satsuma was afraid of repercussions from the Tokugawa, they refused to allow Gesshō into his own domain.

Saigō and Gesshō despaired when they were rebuffed by Satsuma. Saigō may have had a resolute spirit, but he was also driven by emotion. In the end, Gesshō and Saigō tried to kill themselves by jumping from a boat into the ocean. Saigō was saved. Gesshō, however, lost his life.

Saigō was then ordered to go into hiding on the southern island of Amami-Ōshima. How sad I was when I first heard Saigō had committed suicide. So I was really relieved to know he had been saved, even if it meant he had to disappear.

I knew Saigō would someday have to return, because no one else could work so well with the aristocrats in Kyoto. Saigō was the only man looked on with trust and friendship among the influential persons in the imperial court who were doing their best to get along with the Tokugawa government. For example, I was able to marry Iesada thanks to Saigō's effort in Kyoto as part of a special mission from the lord Nariakira.

Saigō's mind had a clear grasp of complexities. He liked the serious and sincere passion of the pro-emperor samurai and activists. On the other hand, he understood the need for there to

THE SECOND STORY

be cooperation between the imperial court and the Tokugawa government.

It was the lord Nariakira who had taught Saigō how important this cooperation was. He told Saigō that if the relationship between the emperor and the shogun were to fracture, our nation would descend into chaos. Then Japan would become a vulnerable target for the Western nations to penetrate into.

Therefore, while Saigō supported the Tokugawa government, he also remained sympathetic to the young patriots who showed sincere respect and reverence toward the age-old status of the imperial line.

The calculations involved here were complex. But Saigō's genius enabled him to deal with the situation. Some people say his innate cleverness turned him into a cunning politician. Well, I think that is not true. I think Saigō was a man who loved passion. He was always moved by others' enthusiasm.

So eventually, Saigō switched his allegiance. After many struggles, he decided to work with Chōshū to overthrow the Tokugawa, for the sake of our nation's future. It was then that Satsuma and Chōshū defeated the Tokugawa in the battle of Toba-Fushimi. It was the winter of 1868. Saigō's change of heart shocked me deeply.

After the first victory, Saigō decided to destroy the Tokugawa by attacking their home base in Edo. But at the last moment he was persuaded not to do so. Instead, he accepted the proposal of a peaceful transfer of power. I believe he was thinking about what might happen to me. And I believe he was also mindful of the late Nariakira's intentions when he sat down at the final negotiation table with the Tokugawa envoy in 1868.

The Third Story

My name is Aikana. I am Saigō's "island wife." In other words, I was Saigō's wife when he was living in exile on the island Amami-Ōshima.

Saigō attempted suicide with Gesshō in 1858. Fortunately he survived. However, the lord of Satsuma was afraid of prosecution by the Tokugawa if Satsuma hid Saigō, who supported pro-emperor activists. The lord decided to send Saigō to a remote island and to put out the story that he was dead.

To deceive the shogunate, Saigō was ordered to adopt a fake name. His boat sailed out from Kagoshima on January 4, 1859. The island Amami-Ōshima is located between Satsuma and the Ryūkyū Kingdom. It is a peaceful and beautiful southern island. From the mainland of Japan, it takes many days to reach.

When I met Saigō, he looked tired after his long trip on the ocean. He still regretted the loss of Gesshō, and he felt guilty that he had somehow survived. Saigō took Gesshō's death hard. Somebody needed to comfort him. I was told by my father to serve Saigō as a wife while he was on our island.

At first I was afraid of Saigō because of his large, piercing eyes. But, when he smiled at me, I sensed he was a really lonely man. Satsuma had abandoned him and now he is on my island where nobody knows who he is.

He called me Aiko-san. And I called him Kichi-san because his real name was Saigō Kichinosuke. (It was only after the era of the Tokugawa shogun ended that he officially changed his name to Takamori.) But as he was in disguise, I could call him Kichi-san only at home.

While Saigō was on our island, he received many letters from his political friends. Some even visited him. I felt quite happy to see Kichi-san gradually recover his mental health. The island life healed his body and soul.

As he grew stronger, he learned to get along with us islanders. Kichi-san was bright. He learned about our island quickly. We were poor islanders suffering from heavy taxation by the lord of Satsuma. Our life depended on sugar cane. And Satsuma needed our sugar cane to produce a lot of revenue. Kichi-san protected us from the bureaucrats. They would come and be merciless in their attempt to collect taxes from us. Kichi-san complained loudly and even threatened to report their mistreatment and cruelty to my lord when he return to the mainland. Kichi-san encouraged us. He educated island children. And he taught island men how to better manage their lives.

Our marriage lasted only three years. In 1860 I heard that there was a big political incident involving the Tokugawa government. For me, such things were too difficult and far away. I learned from Kichi-san, however, that what was happening on the mainland was really important.

According to his friend, Kichi-san told me, the chief minister Ii Naosuke had been assassinated near Edo Castle. And because of that, all prosecutions against the pro-emperor activists had been called off. It meant Kichi-san could

THE THIRD STORY

go back to his homeland. That was good for
him. But it was sad for me. In the feudal era,
an island wife was not allowed to go to the
mainland with her husband.

Kichi-san was ordered to return to the
mainland in January of 1862. By that time, we
had a son and a daughter.

"Now I have to say goodbye," Kichi-san said
to me. "I don't know if we will see each other
again." His big eyes filled with tears.

I smiled and nodded. I stifled my feelings
so as not to upset him and said, "Don't worry, I
will take care of our son and daughter."

I said goodbye to my husband. After he
left, I cried. I really cried, even though he had
kindly left enough money for me to manage
with our children. But oh dear, when my son
Kikujirō turned eight years old, he was adopted
by the main household of Saigō's family. Many
years later, Kikujirō studied in the U.S. and
became quite an important government official.
I am really proud of him. Kikujirō visited me
several times. Whenever I met him, I would
talk about Kichi-san. And Kikujirō would tell

me of Kichi-san's tragic life after leaving our island.

When Kichi-san left Amami-Ōshima, I thought I would never see him again. However, seven months later, I met him again briefly.

To my surprise, he had been exiled a second time. It was while he was on his way to the even-more-distant island of Okino-Erabu that he stopped by our neighbor's place, where I was able to meet him again. He explained why he was facing new charges against him.

I cried for him. Even if I could not understand the politics, I knew he was being unfairly accused. Kichi-san wanted to work hard for Satsuma. But his effort was not rewarded by his new lord. To the contrary, his lord hated what he did.

I still could not understand why he was being treated so harshly.

Within a week, Kichi-san was sent off to Okino-Erabu island, a small, isolated place in the far south. I never saw him again. Many years later, I heard that Kichi-san had married again at Kagoshima, the capital of Satsuma.

THE THIRD STORY

His bride's name was Itoko, and she was the daughter of a high-ranking samurai clan.

I know I can never go to the mainland even if I really want to. This is my fate as an island wife.

The Fourth Story

My name is Ōkubo Toshimichi. I am a long-time friend and political ally of Saigō Takamori.

Let me explain more about why he was exiled a second time. It was I who persuaded my Lord Shimazu Hisamitsu to release Saigō. My lord needed help in achieving his political goal, which was to foster collaboration between the imperial court and the shogunate. The memory of former lord Nariakira was still fresh, and Hisamitsu, right after he became the leader of Satsuma, was anxious to show off his authority. He wanted to go to Edo as soon as possible to make his mark. Saigō was the perfect person to connect my lord to the influential aristocrats at the imperial court.

So Saigō was brought back to Kagoshima from Amami-Ōshima. He advised Lord Hisamitsu not to be in such a hurry. And he went on and on about how great and famous a leader Nariakira had been.

THE FOURTH STORY

Hisamitsu hated to hear such things. So when Saigō made a trip to Kyoto without first getting the lord's permission, Hisamitsu condemned Saigō. Eventually, Saigō was punished and exiled again.

For some reason Lord Hisamitsu and Saigō could not get along with each other. Hisamitsu had an inferiority complex toward his brother Nariakira. But Saigō was too matter-of-fact to consider such feelings a fit subject for conversation. Saigō had been my friend my entire life, and I can attest that he is not someone who beats around the bush. Nariakira liked this quality. However, Lord Hisamitsu felt quite differently.

Saigō and I both came from the poor and low samurai ranks. While Saigō was at Amami-Ōshima, I was given a promotion by Lord Hisamitsu. I really wanted Saigō back in Satsuma so we could work together.

Anyway, as I mentioned, Saigō was arrested and exiled again to a prison on a remote and isolated southern island, Okino-Erabu. The miserable conditions in his cell took a heavy toll on his health. Had the islanders been less sympathetic to him, he would not have survived. But for whatever reason, the islanders liked Saigō, and secretly they made life in his prison cell easier to bear.

During Saigō's absence, many things were happening. Kyoto became a more and more dangerous place, a battlefield for the struggles between the pro-emperor activists and the pro-shogun samurai. Assassinations were a daily event. Above all, the pro-emperor group led by the Chōshū domain persuaded the major aristocrats openly to condemn the weak policy of the Tokugawa government toward the Western powers.

Both Satsuma and Aizu wanted a peaceful relationship between the emperor and shogun. However, many activists dispatched from Chōshū sabotaged our efforts. My lord was quite angered when he learned that many pro-emperor samurai were even operating in Satsuma. So he ordered them purged, and directed that they be attacked and killed at the Terada-ya inn near Kyoto. Then, my lord

THE FOURTH STORY

traveled to Edo to meet the shogun and try to win him over.

However, he could not stay in Edo long because the situation in Kyoto was getting worse and worse. And at the same, Satsuma was facing a serious international problem.

This was in 1862, while Saigō was still suffering as a result of the harsh prison life he had endured on Okino-Erabu island. Unbelievably, Satsuma now had to fight the British! There had

Scene of Anglo-Satsuma War or *Satsu-Ei Sensō*

been an incident on the road back from Edo.
After meeting with the shogun, Hisamitsu's
return route to Satsuma took him through
Kyoto. At one point along the way, his guards
killed and injured some English merchants as
they sat mounted on horses in front of the lord's
procession.

I think this was a sad and unfortunate
accident due to a misunderstanding. In Japan,
under feudal rule, remaining standing in front
of a procession of the lord was considered quite
disrespectful. The English merchants simply
had no understanding of this custom and must
have been frozen with fear when guards ran up
to them with their swords drawn.

To make matters worse, the English pan-
icked and ran straight into the parade route
with their horses. Finally the guards cut them
down with their swords. One of the English
died. Another two were injured.

The British then asked the Tokugawa government to pay compensation, and in retaliation
sent their fleet to Satsuma. I think it was when
the foreign fleet started to attack Kagoshima

THE FOURTH STORY

that the people of Satsuma really understood how they had underestimated Western power. The city was severely damaged by gunfire from the British fleet.

But the samurai in Satsuma fought well and held their own. Even the British soldiers were impressed. After that incident, Satsuma was determined to absorb Western technology and culture. We took a friendly approach to foreign powers, particularly England. We started to send our students to London. We also purchased many advanced weapons from British merchants.

In this new circumstance, Saigō was the only one who could rebuild Satsuma's status in both Edo and Kyoto. Everybody agreed that we needed Saigō to deal with this chaos even if the lord Hisamitsu still hated him.

I decided to support Saigō again. At many people's urging, Hisamitsu reluctantly agreed to bring Saigō back. However, when Saigō was released from his island prison, he was so weak that he could not even stand.

Saigō did not have any time to lose. As soon as he arrived back in Satsuma, he decided he would go to Kyoto at once to deal with the tangled political situation there between the shogun and the emperor.

Now Satsuma's task was to crush the anti-shogun activists in Kyoto. Since the lord of Aizu was quite loyal to the shogun, he wanted to control Kyoto politics more one-sidedly. He created a special police force called the Shinsen-gumi to torture and kill anyone deemed suspicious. Saigō decided to protect the imperial court from such a radical move, but at the same time he was determined to distance himself from the strategies of Aizu, which from his point of view were far too arrogant.

Remember how in the "First Story" Saitō Hajime told what he knew about Saigō? I was skeptical: How could he understand Saigō? Saitō Hajime was working for Aizu. And he was one of the bloodiest soldiers in the Shinsen-gumi. Saigō and I hated them. They were nothing more than violent lowlifes who thought they would get to eat nicer food just by serving the lord of Aizu.

But in the summer of 1864, Satsuma and

Aizu had to work together to protect the Imperial Palace from the troops commanded by Chōshū. Many activists from Chōshū took up arms against us and attempted to break in and gain control of the palace. The lord of Aizu stood against them. He also asked for Satsuma's help.

Saigō did a magnificent job. He successfully protected the emperor and his subordinates. And he swept the enemy out of downtown Kyoto. This was called the Battle of Hamaguri Gate, after the entryway to the Imperial Palace where the fighting took place.

As a result of this battle, almost all the activists from the Chōshū domain were expelled from Kyoto. The Tokugawa shogun, having regained control of the Court, decided to attack the Chōshū domain to punish all the rebels.

The shogun ordered his army to move on Chōshū. Saigō was expected to play an important role in the campaign.

Chōshū was already in big trouble. Right before the Battle of Hamaguri Gate, Shimonoseki, the port town of Chōshū, had

Capture of Chōshū cannons at Shimonoseki

been occupied and destroyed by an allied fleet of British, American, French, and Dutch vessels. This was meant to punish Chōshū for its attacks on Western ships sailing into its territory. Chōshū was of course soundly defeated. Like Satsuma, Chōshū learned its lesson and decided to study and adopt Western technology.

The shogun intended to attack while Chōshū lay weakened from its battle with foreign fleets. Around that time, Saigō met Katsu Kaishū, the top general of the shogun's navy. Saigō said later how greatly impressed he was by the meeting, and that it was an eye-opening moment for him.

THE FOURTH STORY

Katsu is quite smart and straightforward. He is a typical Edo native. When Saigō visited him, he meant to complain to Katsu about how the attitude of Tokugawa was always ambiguous about foreign policy.

But before Saigō began to speak, Katsu jumped in and without any pleasantries immediately asked, "What is the most important thing for you? Satsuma, the emperor, or the shogun?"

"Well, everything is important. We have to coordinate all of them well." Saigō said.

"No, none of these are important," Katsu immediately replied.

Saigō was surprised by Katsu's frank and forthcoming attitude.

"What? Why?" Saigō asked.

Katsu looked at him and said, "Ah, you don't understand. Nothing is more important than our nation, right? For all of us, Japan is the most important thing."

Saigō gazed at Katsu quietly.

"No Western nations care about who is Chōshū or who is Satsuma. They consider us all as Japanese. Shogun? Emperor? While we are arguing about such stupid matters and divided into pro-shogun and pro-emperor factions, Japan will be torn apart by Western powers. What we have to do first and foremost is to make our nation united."

"How?" Saigō mumbled in reply.

"Stop this stupid war. Think about how to get along with Chōshū."

"That is impossible." Saigō said.

"Look. When Satsuma was attacked by the British fleet, you were in exile. But do you think any other domains and lords cared or worried the least little bit?"

"Well …"

"DO YOU KNOW THAT BOTH SATSUMA AND CHŌSHŪ ARE A PART OF JAPAN?"

Saigō was shocked.

Katsu continued: "OK. Now you understand. Chōshū took gunfire from four Western allied powers. Unfortunately, the Tokugawa could not do anything. And now even the shogunate is trying to punish Chōshū. And Aizu and Satsuma both consider what happens in

Chōshū as if it is some other nation's problem. Again, Chōshū is one of the regions of *our* country. We need to integrate ourselves. And you, you are the only man who can do it, Saigō-san."

After a silence, Saigō nodded.

"Work for the future of our nation. For the Tokugawa? For Satsuma? It's a tiny matter. I am working for the shogun. I know my role and responsibility. However, do you know what I really care about? I care about our nation called Japan."

"I understand, Katsu-san." Saigō spoke with deep respect.

"I know many capable and talented men in Chōshū. Talk to them and figure out how to stop these stupid battles."

Yes, this was the last moment of the feudal era. Some people started considering Japan's future as one nation. Still, most of the other samurai could not grasp the big picture. They only thought about their domain and their lord. And beyond their domain, they saw the shogun and emperor as the supreme powers. Nobody thought of Japan as one nation.

Both Saigō and I believed that the emperor and shogun must work together. And we believed this would also be good for Satsuma. Saigō was surprised that Katsu, who was working for shogun, thought and cared more about Japan as a nation than he did about the immediate benefit to his employer.

Saigō decided to broker a peace with Chōshū. In Chōshū, however, everybody hated Satsuma. Because of Saigō, they had lost many colleagues and friends who shared the same belief, that Satsuma and Aizu were backward-thinking enemies who had stuck with the shogun's authority and thus delayed many needed reforms.

After receiving permission from the shogun, Saigō went to the Chōshū domain to start negotiations. It was dangerous for him to visit the enemy's territory. Fanatic Chōshū samurai might kill him.

However, because of the battle against foreign fleets and the loss at the Battle of Hamaguri Gate, Chōshū was in quite a desperate situation.

"We need there to be some agreement between you and the Tokugawa," Saigō said to the top Chōshū official. "Isn't it a good idea to consider what we can compromise on and what we cannot?"

Eventually an agreement was signed. Three top ministers of Chōshū would commit *seppuku* or ritual suicide to take responsibility for the rebellion. And the imperial aristocrats supporting Chōshū would be sent to another domain and confined. Chōshū would also swear allegiance to the Tokugawa shogun.

After meeting with leading scholars in Chōshū, Saigō started to consider what the future of Japan might look like. He shared his thoughts with me and other colleagues in Satsuma. We both agreed that we should not be under the shogun's rule anymore. We could see that the Tokugawa government would never reform our nation. And we believed the current feudal system was an obstacle to creation of a modern state.

So Saitō Hajime of Shinsen-gumi was right to worry. We decided to pretend that we were working with Aizu on the shogun's behalf.

I returned to Satsuma and reported our decision to the lord Hisamitsu. At just this time, Chōshū went through a major political upheaval. The leaders of Satsuma and Chōshū met secretly in Kyoto. Saigō and I were there. We offered weapons and other necessities to Chōshū because their economy was in such a perilous condition. They accepted. This was a huge turn of events.

As we were making a secret alliance with Chōshū, the Tokugawa shogun came to Kyoto and tried to dominate the imperial court again. The shogunate accused Chōshū of being unsupportive. Tokugawa Iemochi, the fourteenth shogun, decided to attack Chōshū again. By then, Katsu Kaishū had lost his position because of some conspiracy inside the Tokugawa government. So there was nobody inside the shogunate who could stop the decision to open hostilities against Chōshū.

Finally the war between Tokugawa and Chōshū broke out. It was 1866. Satsuma did not aid the Tokugawa. Instead, we secretly assisted Chōshū. And Chōshū fought very well. The shogun's army was defeated in the major battles.

"Look. Things are progressing. Let's get going!" I said to Saigō.

"Yes. Now we need to move our nation forward," Saigō replied.

In the middle of the war between the Tokugawa and Chōshū, Iemochi, the fourteenth shogun, died in Osaka. He was only twenty years old. Tokugawa Yoshinobu became the fifteenth shogun. He would be the last shogun of the Tokugawa government. And he was also the last political leader of the samurai era. Yoshinobu ordered Katsu Kaishū to negotiate with Chōshū. He wanted a cease-fire.

Well, I knew it would be a tough mission. Yoshinobu and Katsu did not get along well. From Katsu's point of view, Yoshinobu was too arrogant. Eventually, with the help of the imperial court, both sides withdrew their soldiers.

After this war, the power of the Tokugawa seriously deteriorated. And it was additionally unfortunate for Yoshinobu when Emperor

Kōmei, who had supported the Tokugawa, died in 1867 and Emperor Meiji, who was still young, succeeded the throne.

On our side, in addition to Chōshū, the Tosa domain joined our alliance. The lord of Tosa wrote a petition to Yoshinobu. He asked Yoshinobu to resign from the position of shogun. Yoshinobu agreed.

Maybe Yoshinobu thought that if he resigned, there would be nobody to take on the administrative chores of government. Yoshinobu left Kyoto and moved to Osaka. This marked the end of the feudal rule of the Tokugawa.

Right after Yoshinobu's resignation, we approached the court and obtained an imperial edict that abolished the Tokugawa government and all of Tokugawa Yoshinobu's claims to power. Saigō's connections with leading aristocrats had worked. I and Iwakura Tomomi, who was one of the key aristocrats, created a provisional government with other influential lords.

Once the formal edict was announced, many

THE FOURTH STORY

lords who had just been observing the situation without taking sides decided to declare their allegiance to the imperial court. Thus, the Restoration of Emperor Meiji was officially announced.

In January of 1868, the Tokugawa army and the allied army of the new imperial government led by Saigō went to war in Toba and Fushimi, suburbs of Kyoto. After three days of bloody battle, our side won. Yoshinobu retreated from Osaka to Edo with the lord of Aizu.

"I will attack Edo." Saigō said.

"Yes, we need to destroy the old system. To do it, the Tokugawa must be eliminated."

Both Saigō and I were determined to abolish the Tokugawa. But both of us were wondering about Tenshō-In.

"Do you know how we can save her life?" Saigō asked.

Saigō and I had known Tenshō-In since she was a small child. She left Satsuma to become the wife of the thirteenth shogun in 1856.

"It was the late lord Nariakira who arranged her marriage. I do not want her to get hurt. And we cannot harm the imperial princess Kazuno-miya, either," Saigō repeated.

Kazuno-miya, the sister of the last emperor, had married Tokugawa Iemochi, the fourteenth shogun. Such personal concerns made attacking Edo quite a tough decision. Saigō, however, was determined to manage all these delicate matters.

Taisei Hōkan or the restoration of Imperial rule

The Fifth Story

I am Katsu Kaishū. I owe Saigō Takamori a great deal. Indeed, he was the greatest general of our time.

Edo was saved because of him. When the new imperial government accused Yoshinobu, the last shogun, of treason, the pro-Tokugawa samurai decided to fight against Satsuma and Chōshū. From their point of view, Satsuma and Chōshū were traitors who had manipulated the emperor. They could not understand why Yoshinobu and his loyalists were now being called the rebels instead.

Everybody assumed that any battle between the Tokugawa and the allied army of Satsuma-Chōshū would take place in Edo. I myself did not get along with Yoshinobu, but my family had served the Tokugawa for hundreds of years. I at least wanted to try to save the Tokugawa clan as well as the city of Edo, home to more than a million people.

THE FIFTH STORY

So when the Imperial Army drew closer to Edo, I decided to parley with Saigō to avoid war. Yoshinobu had already stated he would obey the new government. But it seemed impossible to tame the fanatic samurai who were opposed to it.

Tenshō-In sent a letter to Saigō and asked him not to attack Edo Castle. And she asked me to talk to Saigō and his men. I sent Yamaoka Tesshū to see Saigō, who had already arrived at Shizuoka, near Mt. Fuji, which was close enough to be visible from Edo. Saigō appreciated my communication. I decided to meet with him directly when he arrived in Edo.

If Saigō Takamori had not been the one with whom I negotiated, Edo would have been reduced to ashes. Think about it. If Edo is the battlefield, Japan falls into a catastrophic civil war, and our nation is destroyed. By whatever means necessary, I wanted to avoid this battle.

I visited Saigō's office as the formal envoy of the Tokugawa. To my surprise, he did not treat me like some defeated enemy. From the beginning to the end of our negotiations, he treated me with respect. He did not challenge me at all. He was always quiet. He was not the least bit arrogant.

The last minutes of our discussion were filled with friendly exchanges.

"Katsu-san, I will take care of it. Please do not worry."

"I appreciate it."

"And, how are Tenshō-In and Kazuno-miya doing? Above all, Tenshō-In must worried and dismayed by this outcome."

"Don't worry. She trusts you. She and Kazuno-miya are fine. I believe they will be leaving Edo Castle soon."

"Katsu-san, I learned a lot from you. This is the time for me to pay it back."

Edo was saved.

I left Saigō's office without incident. I was so surprised, because it did not take more than an hour before all the deployments of the Imperial Army came to a halt. Edo and its surroundings became quiet, just like a calm ocean. I was amazed at the extent of Saigō's influence over his army.

THE FIFTH STORY

A week later, the Imperial Army marched into Edo without any disruption. Edo Castle was handed over to Saigō's forces in early April of 1868.

Now I have something else to tell you. From the outset of this conflict, the French government had always supported the Tokugawa. Our navy was much more powerful than that of the new imperial government. It was interesting that the French ambassador tried to persuade Yoshinobu to fight back. I knew that the French hated the British, who were supporting the emperor. And in the middle were the Americans, trying to sell as many weapons as they could to the Japanese because the Civil War had ended in the U.S. and there was a surplus of guns left over that now needed to be gotten rid of.

I did not want to see Japan so much under the influence of these Western powers. I knew what had happened in China, India, and many other nations. So both Saigō and I agreed to weigh the benefits to Japan, as we had in our discussions in Kyoto some years ago.

Indeed, Saigō was not my enemy. We held many ideas in common. But we also held very different positions in our respective governments.

My family had been serving the shogun many years. How could I just betray my master and become a toady for his rival? At the same time I believed our country must be reformed and modernized for the sake of our future. I knew my task was quite tough. And it was my fate to deal with it.

After Edo Castle was handed over, I met Saigō again.

"Katsu-san," he told me, "I am relieved that Edo will be all right, thanks to you. I leave it in your hands. I will mention to Ōkubo that you will handle things here."

"But your presence in Edo is vital. Please stay here with us."

Saigō said he had to go to northern Japan, where many pro-Tokugawa lords were still resisting. The lord of Aizu was one of the most persistent enemies in that area.

When Saigō and I had dinner together, I

remember he mentioned how much he had
liked the island life. I know he missed his days
on Amami-Ōshima with Aikana.

Yes. Saigō always said he wanted to live
like a farmer. He loved hunting. He loved to
plow and to hoe. You know? Saigō was not a
heavy drinker at all. He got drunk far too easily.
Instead, Saigō liked sweets. But when we were
talking that time, he was drunk and his face was
red. I remember him whispering to me that he
preferred the smell of the cesspool at his home
to the incense at a high-ranking residence. And
then he laughed like a child.

Me? I never consider staying in the countryside. I am an Edo city boy. But, I understand
Saigō's feeling. I think he sometimes was really
tired of politics.

"Have you ever visited Satsuma?" Saigō
asked me.

I had not, but I did go there later to
negotiate with Lord Hisamitsu and secure his
cooperation with the new government.

"Satsuma is a beautiful place," Saigō went
on. "The climate is warm and the people

modest. At the head of the city, you will see Sakurajima volcano looming over the bay. It is an active volcano, and we often hear the sound of eruptions. I will invite you to my house when you're in Kagoshima. Our food is quite plain, but I believe you will enjoy it. I will serve you *Satsuma shōchū*, which we distill from sweet potato. After our government gains full control, I want to retire and enjoy life back there. Once everything is over, let's get together at my home."

Unfortunately, this would never happen. The tragic end to Saigō's life made it impossible.

The series of rebellions against the new government continued until the summer of 1869. First there was the fight on the hill at Ueno in Edo. That lasted only a day. After this, the Tokugawa supporters went north, where the lord of Aizu was still working against the new government.

After a few brutal battles, Aizu finally surrendered in November. The rest of the pro-Tokugawa rebels retreated to Hakodate on Hokkaido. But they were destroyed in June of 1869. Japan had been saved and reunited again.

THE FIFTH STORY

The series of battles between 1868 and 1869 is called the War of Boshin after the name of the year on the traditional calendar.

My task now was how to save Edo. Edo had been spared gunfire. But Edo was not yet safe from financial crisis.

Edo had been the main administrative city of the Tokugawa shogunate for 265 years. You can imagine how many people worked directly or indirectly for the government there. After the shogun was gone, Edo was about to become flooded with the unemployed. Saigō said I would be able to manage things in Edo. But you know, it is not so easy. Not easy at all, Saigō-san.

So I then met with Ōkubo Toshimichi. He was Saigō's best friend and a quite capable politician in the new imperial government. Ōkubo said the best way to save Edo is to make the city the capital of Japan. Of course. That was a brilliant idea.

On September 3, 1868, Edo was renamed Tokyo. Tokyo means "Eastern Capital," in contrast to Kyoto to the west, which had been Japan's capital for more than a thousand years.

59

On October 13, the emperor arrived to take up residence in the new capital of Tokyo. A new Imperial Palace was build inside Edo Castle, which had been the shogun's headquarters. Now, Edo—Tokyo—had been saved again. The city quickly became the political and economic capital of Japan.

After the war was over, Saigō Takamori returned to Satsuma and lived with his family. He enjoyed farming and hunting.

But in Tokyo, no one could afford to rest, because there were so many things for the new government to attend to. Japan had to transition from a feudal nation divided by lords and their domains to a modern nation under a centralized government. The people who had made the Meiji Restoration possible were samurai. Yet through their reforms they came to abolish the very society they had ruled over for many many years. In other words, they had to fundamentally change the systems, customs, and privileges whose benefits they had all been enjoying.

Unfortunately, it seemed that the new

government was too weak to carry out these tough tasks.

First of all, many people complained that only Satsuma and Chōshū held power in the new government. Secondly, farmers were suffering from the heavy taxes required to rebuild the nation. And within the government itself, the radical reformers and conservatives argued and confronted each other.

Kido Kōin from Chōshū, Iwakura Tomomi from the imperial court, and Ōkubo Toshimichi from Satsuma were the three men at the top who managed governmental affairs. But there were great differences among them over strategy.

I think Ōkubo was a smart politician. However, he hated to move ahead quickly. He was a rather prudent leader. Kido was an idealist. He really wanted drastic change. Iwakura was not a samurai, but he was part of the nobility and a talented tactician. If all of them pooled their strengths to create a kind of synergy, there might be real progress. But the reality was different. Their respective talents clashed and brought a halt to the movement toward reformation.

Human beings are complex. Everybody has pride. Once pride meets pride, the situation gets quite tangled indeed. What these men needed was a moderate presence, someone who could facilitate their discussions.

The key factor to understand is that Japan was still under the control of its old feudal system. The samurai were warriors who served their lords. Like the shogun, who was the lord of lords, all lords had samurai loyal to them within their respective domains or fiefs, called "han." Each han maintained its own military and administrative system. So to create a new, modern government under the authority of the emperor, Japan had to first get rid of this domain structure, and it had to do so as quickly as possible.

This demanded strong leadership, but as I mentioned, the government leaders were not up to the task. In the end, they called on Saigō once again.

It was in December of 1871 that Saigō

THE FIFTH STORY

returned to Tokyo. Under his leadership and pledge of military support, all the lords agreed to give up their privileges and hand their domains over to the government. The han system was abolished. Domains were converted to prefectures, and each prefecture had its governor appointed by the central government in Tokyo.

After instituting these reforms, Iwakura, Kido, and Ōkubo set off on an official mission to visit the Western nations and establish formal diplomatic relations. It was a long trip. They were gone from Japan for almost two years. During their absence, Saigō took a leadership position in the government.

Well, I watched what he did. He even asked me for help. But I hated to formally join the new government because I had been working for the shogun. I had to keep my pride as a former samurai. Of course, I gave advice when asked. And I sometimes I received an appointment to one position or another. But I always resigned after a short time.

During the other leaders' absence, Saigō

made many important reforms. He established the police force. He shaped the judiciary, education, and military systems. Since 1612, Christianity had been illegal in Japan. Saigō rescinded that law so that Japan could work with the Christian nations of the West.

In the years after the Meiji Restoration, people began adopting modern hair styles. Many samurai stopped carrying swords. Saigō's government strongly supported such transformations. Within a few years, Japan had utterly changed. In 1873, the government began a military draft system. Until then, only a samurai could be considered a soldier. Now anybody could put on a military uniform.

Unfortunately, all these changes injured the pride of the samurai. There were no samurai in the Meiji era. Frustrated, the samurai complained: "We worked hard to change our nation. But for what?" They had lost all their privileges, jobs, status, honor, and pride. They felt the government had betrayed them.

Look. What Saigō did was great. But at the same time, he must have felt sorry for how the

THE FIFTH STORY

former samurai were suffering. He knew he had to change Japanese society. And he knew at the same that if he did so, the people from the samurai class would be hurt. I believed this regret eventually got the better of Saigō himself.

And so it was unfortunate that, when Saigō was still in charge of the government, the so-called "Korean Issue" developed. Our delegation of leaders came back from abroad to deal with this problem and ended up clashing with Saigō over strategy. Saigō wanted to establish relations with Korea. The others were opposed and did not want Saigō to engage in any diplomatic efforts.

They argued. Things got very intense. I remember this as the starting point of Saigō's tragic downfall.

The Sixth Story

My name is Itō Hirobumi.

In 1885, I became the first prime minister under Japan's new constitution. Since Saigō's death, all the rebellions and battles against the government have completely come to an end. Japan has gradually become more like the other advanced nations in Europe. Now, if people have a grievance, they launch a political campaign!

I am from Chōshū. I vividly recall how in 1860 Japan was facing serious challenges. Major Western powers were asking Japan to open its ports for trading. Could the Japanese survive without giving up their independence to other nations?

In Chōshū, there was a private school called Shōka-Son Juku. We often met there to brainstorm, and we came up with countless ways of dealing with this chaotic situation. Many young intellectuals openly expressed their opinion that the Japanese feudal government had neither

THE SIXTH STORY

enough ability nor the right leadership. The existing political system was worn out and beyond repair. We argued whether even we Chōshū samurai had enough strength to stand up and fight against the foreign threat.

Many people expressed the opinion that before we could take on the Western nations, we had to first learn their technology and systems. I agreed with them. So I promoted the idea that I should take the opportunity to travel overseas to learn.

But other people insisted that Japan must arm itself with the power of the samurai spirit and reject Western influence outright. To do this, they said, we had to unite under the emperor, not the shogun.

At that time, as in Chōshū, a storm of nationalism was spreading all over the nation. Japan had been isolated from the rest of the world for many years, but now its people were starting to fight among each other to determine the future of their island nation.

I was a typical activist in the center of that storm.

The lord of Chōshū accepted my proposal. I visited London to study Western culture in 1863.

When I arrived there, I saw how advanced the Western nations were. I also discovered how their social organizations had been able to produce such effective technologies and systems for banking and commerce. After returning to Japan, I insisted that we avoid conflict with other countries and instead put our efforts into making Japan more efficient and technologically and financially strong.

And then, so many things happened. The Tokugawa government came to an end in 1868. When the new government was established, my ability to speak English was of value, and I was invited to join.

In 1871, I visited the West again with other leaders of the new Japanese government. Ōkubo, Kido, and Iwakura were with me. When we visited Germany, I met Bismarck, the Chancellor of Germany. I was really impressed by him.

I thought the German constitution would be

a good model for the new Japanese constitution we would have to create. We did not yet know as much as we needed to, and I felt strongly that we needed to concentrate on improving our domestic infrastructure and social system.

When I returned to Japan from my mission, I found members of the government immersed in a fierce argument over diplomacy. Many argued in favor of sending in our troops to punish Korea. What a stupid idea that was! We had to do a lot of other things before flexing our muscles abroad.

Saigō was head of the government at that time. He hoped to manage the problem. But he could not. Eventually, he resigned from his office as chief minister.

People said that Saigō resigned because it was he who insisted on going to war against Korea. That is not true at all.

While Saigō was in office, he tried to open diplomatic relations with the Korean kingdom. But Korea did not accept the Japanese envoy.

In fact, Korea had been deliberately closing its door to the rest of the world. Korea rejected

Western influence. The Koreans were angry to see the Japanese embrace the policy of absorbing Western culture.

Japanese officials were insulted when Korea ignored their entreaties. So they asked Japan to punish Korea in retaliation. But Saigō was opposed to the use of force. He wanted to pursue a diplomatic solution.

When Ōkubo, Kido, and Iwakura came back from their overseas mission, they also wanted solve this problem without using the military. I totally agreed with them.

Saigō then insisted that he personally would visit Korea to negotiate. However, his proposal was turned down.

I didn't think it was a good idea and opposed it, too. If Saigō visited Korea and his negotiations were not successful, there was a big risk of war because Saigō occupied the highest rank in the Japanese government. More important, I thought that we just needed to stay away from diplomatic controversy and concentrate on our pressing domestic issues.

When his proposal to go to Korea was

turned down, Saigō resigned his position in the government. However, when he did so, many discontented samurai tried to turn Saigō into the symbolic leader of their own anti-government movement.

The frustration of the former samurai had long been a serious political issue. Particularly when the government started the military draft system many former samurai took it as an affront to their pride. Their complaints were echoed widely even within the chambers of government itself.

Many samurai said the government had deserted them and let them down. Had they not fought against the Tokugawa? Had the

Samurais from Chōshū, during the Boshin War period

brave soldiers from Satsuma and Chōshū not fought in the War of Boshin? A movement began to exert pressure and make demands for the fair treatment of former samurai.

So when Saigō stepped down in 1873, countless soldiers, especially those from Satsuma, resigned from the military. Many government officials followed them.

Ōkubo was quite disappointed by all this. He was, after all, a man who was always looking for a balanced approach. In his view, Saigō's action was far too emotional and not well thought out. Saigō was his best friend and a political comrade. But when Saigō left Tokyo, their long-time bond was broken, even if Ōkubo thought Saigō had resigned more to deflect the frustrations of the anti-government movement.

Saigō had a younger brother who held a high rank in the Imperial Army. His name was Saigō Tsugumichi. I went to meet him because I wanted him at least to remain in the government.

"Itō-san, please do not worry," he said. "When my brother left Tokyo, he urged me to stay on. My brother persuaded me to take on his role at the military and within the government. Maybe he expected terrible things would befall him after he resigned."

"Indeed, when your brother resigned, he already had a good idea of what would happen," I said to Tsugumichi.

"I believe my brother thought, to achieve reform, somebody had to deal with the wave of discontent among the former samurai class."

Well, I agree that Saigō was one of the leaders who helped reform the nation. And he was also a tragic hero who died with samurai spirit. In other words, he may have opened the door to Japan's modern era, but he died for his nostalgic attachment to the traditional philosophy of the samurai warrior.

After returning to Satsuma, Saigō opened a private school to educate youth. Around that time, frustrated samurai had turned to open rebellion. There were battles and turmoil in Hagi of Chōshū, Saga, Akizuki, Fukuoka and Kumamoto in Kyushu.

Beset by this turbulence, many frustrated

people came to visit Saigō. Gradually his school became the political center of anti-government forces. Of course, the government was monitoring this situation closely. They sent a mission to persuade Saigō to control his students. But Saigō offered nothing in reply.

Katsu also tried to solve the problem. His plan was to ask the former lord Hisamitsu to persuade Saigō to get his students to calm down. Hisamitsu still wore the traditional hairstyle and dressed like a lord of the Tokugawa era. He was unhappy with the turn of events. I suspect he had wanted to be the next leader after the Tokugawa Shogun, but he had been too far out of the loop of the new government administrators. Even his domain of Satsuma had been taken away. Despite receiving an honorable status and considerable money, Hisamitsu felt he was simply being used to smooth things over. Hisamitsu was not comfortable with the idea of talking to Saigō.

It all happened when Saigō was out enjoying a hunting trip in the mountains in the winter of 1877. Some fanatic students and followers

THE SIXTH STORY

had come across a bit of espionage from the government and thought agents were coming to Kagoshima to assassinate Saigō. The students become quite agitated and attacked the warehouse where the government's weapons and bullets were stored.

When Saigō heard the news, he reacted with sincere regret. "But what can I do?" he said to himself.

Saigō never denounced his students who had taken such reckless action. He simply could not abandon his students and followers. And if his students were at fault, didn't that mean that he was at fault?

"Don't worry." Saigō said to them. "I will be with you and take care of you."

It was February 17, 1877. Saigō rose up with his followers.

The Seventh Story

My name is Tatsumi Naofumi. I was a samurai of the Kuwana domain near Nagoya.

My lord was the brother of the lord of Aizu. Around the end of Tokugawa rule, we were stationed in Kyoto and keeping an eye out on the movements of Satsuma and Chōshū.

Sometimes, we worked with the Shinsen-gumi to arrest suspicious men. So I knew all about Saitō Hajime and other key members of the Shinsen-gumi. Saitō was a tough warrior. He was one of the most feared swordsmen of his time.

After Tokugawa Yoshinobu stepped down, I continued to work against the new government.

In the War of Boshin, I went to the Nagaoka domain to help in their resistance. I killed countless soldiers of the new government with my own sword. So when the war ended, I was arrested and spent some time in prison.

After my release, I wondered what to do. I

hated the idea of being a merchant. And I was not interested in teaching children. I did not want to be a boring bureaucrat and push papers all day long for my former enemy.

In the end, I became a police officer. In the old days, there was no difference between soldiers and police. They were both jobs for a samurai. I still was reluctant to work for Satsuma and Chōshū. But what else could I do?

Saitō Hajime was also in the police department. Many of his Shinsen-gumi colleagues had already lost their lives during the time around the War of Boshin. Both Saitō and I were similar: homeless dogs or miserable survivors who had missed our chance for an honorable death.

However, some quite interesting things were happening. In 1873, the government split over its international strategy. Many from Satsuma left Tokyo to become a counterforce opposed to the government. In no time, the government promoted Saitō and me because they needed professional soldiers like us to prepare battle plans against the new rebels. It was just like a revolving door. Former winners were leaving as former losers like us were seeing their careers advance.

Both Saitō Hajime and I joined the War of Seinan and helped defeat Saigō's rebel army. Don't forget that both Saitō and I had been pro-Tokugawa supporters.

Little did I know that Saigō would become my enemy again. After all, he had risen to the top and become the very symbol of the Meiji government.

You can imagine, then, how thrilled I was in 1877 to discover I was now to engage in battle against Saigō's army. Now, the former winners had become the rebels! And I am serving the cause of those who intend to beat them! What a delicious revenge for me! I respected Saigō as a person. But I hated his forces who had defeated us last time. Now they will be my enemy again! Isn't that an ironic turn?

I did not hesitate one minute to join the Imperial Army to fight at the War of Seinan.

As much as I was looking forward to my revenge, I was well aware that Saigō was quite a popular figure in Japan. Still, great a man as he was, I would enjoy taking him down, because for many times in my life, he had been my arch-enemy.

I believed deeply in the tradition of the samurai. Samurai were the warriors of Japan and as a class had dominated our nation for almost 800 years. They were proud servants of their lords and shogun.

However, in 1868, everything changed. The allied forces under the imperial court overthrew the government of the Tokugawa Shogun. They abolished the feudal system. Saigō was one of the chief architects of this transformation. Under his leadership, the old system was gone. The samurai class was in ruins. And so I was ruined. I know Saigō felt sorry about all the pain he had caused. But it was I who had suffered, and I could not easily forgive him.

The War of Seinan was bloody. Saigō's army attacked Kumamoto Castle first, the local head-quarters of the new government. After losing in Kumamoto, their army gradually went down to defeat. Battles in central Kyushu were fierce.

Government troops embarking at Yokohama to fight the Satsuma rebellion, or war of Seinan

Saitō was hit by a bullet there. Fortunately the wound was not fatal.

Faced with our material superiority, the rebels found themselves cornered in southern Kyushu. By September they had been pushed back to Kagoshima, Satsuma's capital. I was the one who crushed the remaining rebels at the final battle. Soon after, we found Saigō already dead....

Twenty-eight years later, I was near Mukden in Manchuria as one of the divisional commanders of the Imperial Army. A week ago, as a lieutenant general, I had been under severe attack by the Russian army. Japan was at war with Russia in 1904 and 1905. My senior officer, Ōyama Iwao, was actually the younger cousin of Saigō Takamori. Ōyama and I worked together to win this war with Russia. And whenever I saw General Ōyama, I remembered Saigō. Saigō may have been my enemy, but I loved him as an enemy and I could not forget him.

The Russo-Japanese war came to an end thanks to the mediation of Theodore Roosevelt, the president of the U.S. By then we were utterly exhausted and had barely eked out a victory.

Thirty-six years ago, when the Tokugawa shogun gave up his power, Japan was a tiny, underdeveloped country. In but a short period of time thereafter, we created a strong nation that was capable of waging war against a Western superpower.

The contributions of Saigō's cousin Ōyama, as well as Saigō Tsugumichi, his younger brother, were indispensable to our victory over Russia. Perhaps the spirit of Saigō was still among them and among us.

The Last Story

My name is Itoko, the wife of Saigō Takamori.
I married him in 1865. I then adopted Kikujirō
from Aikana, Takamori's "island wife" from his
days in exile.

I was relieved when the government formally
forgave Takamori in 1889. I know the Emperor
Meiji had liked Takamori very much, even
though he had taken up arms against the
government.

Katsu Kaishū and many other important
figures in Japan were eager to repair Takamori's
reputation. When the Meiji constitution was
proclaimed, the government provided a grant of
amnesty and so Takamori's honor was officially
restored.

Just recently, I received a letter from Katsu
Kaishū. He wrote that Takamori's statue would
be installed near Ueno Station in Tokyo. Katsu-
san has been always good to me. He also took
good care of Tenshō-In, the widow of the

thirteenth shogun. She died in 1883.

By the way, Ōkubo Toshimichi was assassinated the year after my husband's death. The killers were former samurai. Lots of people said that before the War of Seinan, Ōkubo and Takamori hated each other. I don't think that's true.

I heard that when Ōkubo was told of my husband's death, he cried out again and again. These two men were friends.

Many people have passed away. Everything began when Commodore Perry came. And when Takamori died at the War of Seinan, everything was over. The people who lived in that era are gradually dying out.

Katsu invited me to the unveiling ceremony of Takamori's statue. It was December of 1898. When I saw it, I wondered if it was a good likeness or not. I know he often liked to take his dog for a walk. But when he was out of doors, he would not be wearing such a casual kimono. Maybe the statue is a bit more like his appearance when he went hunting in the mountains of Kagoshima.

His real face was a little bit different too. But Takamori's big eyes and thick lips are just right.

"Katsu-san, was he really like that?" I asked.

"Don't say that in public. But I agree with you," Katsu whispered. "Well, time goes so fast. Now our era is gone. Maybe this statue of Saigō-san will be the image of him that is handed over to the next generations. For us, he lives inside us. And our memories cannot be forwarded on to those who come after. You know, that's life. It is the nature of human beings."

Katsu Kaishū died the following year.

END

注記

　本書は西郷隆盛の伝記物語を通して、英文で日本史上の過渡期と呼ばれた明治維新前後を解説したものです。ストーリー化したやさしい英文で語る上で、あまりにも複雑と思われる事実はあえて単純に解説してあります。

　たとえば、島津久光は国父と呼ばれ、島津斉彬の死後、薩摩藩の大名として家督を継いだのは、久光の実子の島津忠義でした。しかし、ここではその詳細を省き、最も影響力のあった久光を lord として記載しました。

　また、大名と藩の制度改革には、版籍奉還から廃藩置県への２段階のプロセスがありますが、ここではそれを一つの改革として、詳細を省きました。また、明治維新での様々な改革もすべては記してはいません。

　その他にも、事実の省略、編集箇所がありますので、ご承知おきいただきますよう、お願い致します。

Word List

- LEVEL 1, 2は本文で使われている全ての語を掲載しています。
  LEVEL 3以上は、中学校レベルの語を含みません。ただし、本文で特殊な
  意味で使われている場合、その意味のみを掲載しています。
- 語形が規則変化する語の見出しは原形で示しています。不規則変化語は本文
  中で使われている形になっています。
- 一般的な意味を紹介していますので、一部の語で本文で実際に使われている
  品詞や意味と合っていないことがあります。
- 品詞は以下のように示しています。

名 名詞	代 代名詞	形 形容詞	副 副詞	動 動詞	助 助動詞
前 前置詞	接 接続詞	間 間投詞	冠 冠詞	略 略語	俗 俗語
熟 熟語	頭 接頭語	尾 接尾語	記 記号	関 関係代名詞

A

□ **abandon** 動 ①捨てる，放棄する
②（計画などを）中止する，断念する

□ **ability** 名 ①できること，(〜する)
能力 ②才能

□ **abolish** 動 廃止する，撤廃する

□ **about to** 《be-》まさに〜しよう
としている，〜するところだ

□ **above all** 何よりも

□ **absence** 名 欠席，欠如，不在

□ **absolute** 形 ①完全な，絶対の ②
無条件の

□ **absorb** 動 吸収する

□ **accept** 動 ①受け入れる ②同意す
る，認める

□ **accident** 名 ①（不慮の）事故，災
難 ②偶然

□ **accomplishment** 名 ①完成，達
成 ②業績

□ **according** 副 《-to〜》〜によれ
ば［よると］

□ **accuse** 動 〜に責任を問う，〜を非
難する

□ **achieve** 動 成し遂げる，達成する，
成功を収める **help in achieving 〜**
〜を達成するのに役立つ

□ **active** 形 活動中の **active volcano**

活火山

□ **activist** 名 活動家，実践主義者

□ **activity** 名 活動

□ **actual** 形 実際の，現実の

□ **actually** 副 実際に，本当に，実は

□ **addition** 名 付加，追加 **in
addition to** 〜に加えて

□ **additionally** 副 その上

□ **administrative** 形 ①行政
の ②管理の，運営［経営］上の
administrative chore 管理業務
administrative system 行政機関

□ **administrator** 名 経営者，理事，
管理者 **government administrator**
行政官

□ **adopt** 動 ①採択する，選ぶ ②承認
する ③養子にする

□ **advance** 名 進歩，前進

□ **advanced** 形 上級の，先に進んだ，
高等の

□ **advice** 名 忠告，助言，意見

□ **advise** 動 忠告する，勧める

□ **affairs** 名 業務，仕事，やるべきこと
international affairs 国際情勢

□ **afford** 動 〜する余裕がある

□ **affront** 名 侮辱

□ **afraid of** 《be-》〜を恐れる，〜を

WORD LIST

怖がる

- □ **after all** やはり，結局
- □ **age-old** 形 古い，長い年月を経た
- □ **agent** 名 ①代理人 ②代表者
- □ **agitated** 形 ①かき乱された ②興奮した
- □ **agreement** 名 合意，協定
- □ **ah** 間《驚き・悲しみ・賞賛などを表して》ああ，やっぱり
- □ **aid** 動 援助する，助ける，手伝う
- □ **Aikana** 名 愛加那《西郷隆盛が安政の大獄により，奄美大島に流罪となった時の島妻，1837–1902》
- □ **Aiko** 名 愛子《西郷隆盛が安政の大獄により，奄美大島に流罪となった時の島妻，愛加那の日本名，1837–1902》
- □ **Aizu** 名 会津藩
- □ **Akizuki** 名 秋月の乱《1876年（明治9年）に福岡県秋月（現・福岡県朝倉市秋月）で起こった，明治政府に対する士族反乱》
- □ **all** 熟 above all 何よりも after all やはり，結局 all day long 一日中，終日 all over ～中で，全体に亘って，～の至る所で，全て終わって all right 大丈夫で first of all まず第一に one and all すべての人 not ～ at all 少しも［全然］～ない
- □ **all-powerful** 形 全能の，全権を有する
- □ **allegiance** 名 （君主への）忠誠，献身
- □ **alliance** 名 同盟［国］，協調
- □ **allied** 形 同盟［連合］した，関連した
- □ **allow** 動 ①許す，《– … to ～》…が～するのを可能にする，…に～させておく ②与える
- □ **ally** 名 同盟国，味方
- □ **Amami-Ōshima** 名 奄美大島
- □ **amaze** 動 びっくりさせる，驚嘆させる
- □ **ambassador** 名 大使，使節

- □ **ambiguous** 形 あいまいな，不明瞭な
- □ **ambition** 名 野心
- □ **American** 形 アメリカ（人）の 名 アメリカ人
- □ **amnesty** 名 恩赦
- □ **anger** 動 怒る，～を怒らせる
- □ **announce** 動 （人に）知らせる，公表する
- □ **anti-** 頭 反～，対～《反対，敵対，対抗を表す》
- □ **anxious** 形 ①心配な，不安な ②切望して
- □ **anybody** 代 ①《疑問文・条件節で》誰か ②《否定文で》誰も（～ない）③《肯定文で》誰でも
- □ **anymore** 副 《通例否定文，疑問文で》今はもう，これ以上，これから
- □ **anyone** 代 ①《疑問文・条件節で》誰か ②《否定文で》誰も（～ない）③《肯定文で》誰でも
- □ **anyway** 副 ①いずれにせよ，ともかく ②どんな方法でも
- □ **apart** 副 ばらばらに，離れて torn apart 引き裂かれる
- □ **appearance** 名 外見，印象
- □ **appoint** 動 任命する，指名する
- □ **appointment** 名 任命，指名
- □ **appreciate** 動 ありがたく思う
- □ **approach** 名 アプローチ，接近，（～へ）近づく道
- □ **arch-enemy** 名 最大の敵
- □ **architect** 名 建築家，設計者
- □ **argue** 動 論じる，議論する
- □ **argument** 名 議論，論争
- □ **aristocrat** 名 貴族，特権階級の人
- □ **arm** 動 武装する
- □ **army** 名 軍隊 Imperial Army 官軍 rebel army 反乱軍
- □ **arrange** 動 ①並べる，整える ②取り決める ③準備する，手はずを整える

SAIGŌ TAKAMORI

□ **arrest** 動 逮捕する

□ **arrival** 名 ①到着 ②到達

□ **arrogant** 形 尊大な, 傲慢な, 無礼な, 横柄な

□ **as** 熟 as ~ as one can できる限り ~ as ~ as possible できるだけ~ as a result その結果（として） as a result of ~の結果（として） as if あたかも~のように, まるで~みたいに as much as ~と同じだけ as soon as ~するとすぐ, ~するや否や as well as ~と同様に be known as ~として知られている

□ **ash** 名 灰, 燃えかす be reduced to ashes 焼けて灰になる

□ **Asia** 名 アジア

□ **assassinate** 動 暗殺する

□ **assassination** 名 暗殺

□ **assist** 動 手伝う, 援助する

□ **assume** 動 当然のことと思う

□ **Atsuko** 名 篤子《第13代将軍徳川家定の正室, 1836–1883》

□ **attachment** 名 愛着

□ **attack** 動 襲う, 攻める 名 攻撃

□ **attempt** 動 試みる, 企てる 名 試み, 企て

□ **attend to** 動 ~に注意を払う, 専念する, ~の世話をする

□ **attest** 動 （真実であることを）証言[証明]する

□ **attitude** 名 姿勢, 態度, 心構え

□ **authority** 名 権威, 権力, 権限

□ **avoid** 動 避ける, （~を）しないようにする

□ **aware** 形 ①気がついて, 知って ②（~の）認識のある

B

□ **background** 名 背景, 前歴, 生い立ち

□ **backward-thinking** 形 保守的

［後ろ向き］な考え方の

□ **balanced** 形 釣り合いのとれた

□ **banking** 名 銀行業

□ **barbarian** 名 野蛮人, 未開人

□ **barely** 副 かろうじて, やっと

□ **base** 名 基礎, 土台, 本部 home base 本拠地

□ **basically** 副 基本的には, 大筋では

□ **battle** 名 戦闘, 戦い

□ **battlefield** 名 戦場

□ **battleship** 名 戦艦

□ **bear** 動 耐える

□ **beat** 動 ①打つ ②打ち負かす beat around the bush 遠回しな［回りくどい］言い方をする

□ **befall** 動 （災害などが）~に起こる, 降りかかる

□ **beginning** 名 初め, 始まり

□ **behalf** 名 利益 on one's behalf ~のために

□ **behavior** 名 振る舞い, 態度, 行動

□ **being** 名 存在, 生命, 人間 human being 人, 人間

□ **belief** 名 信じること, 信念, 信用

□ **belong** 動 《- to ~》~に属する, ~のものである

□ **benefit** 名 利益, 恩恵 動 利益を得る, （~の）ためになる

□ **Beppu** 名 別府晋介《幕末から明治初期の武士（薩摩藩士）, 軍人。西郷を介錯した, 1847–1877》

□ **beset by** ~に苦しむ, 悩まされる

□ **best** 熟 do one's best 全力を尽くす

□ **betray** 動 裏切る, 背く, だます

□ **beyond** 前 ~を越えて, ~の向こうに

□ **Bismarck** 名 （オットー・フォン・）ビスマルク《Otto von Bismarck, プロイセン王国とドイツ帝国の宰相, 1815–1898》

□ **bit** 名 ①小片, 少量 ②《a –》少し,

WORD LIST

ちょっと

- □ **bloody** 形 血だらけの, 血なまぐさい, むごい
- □ **bond** 名 結びつき, 結束, 絆
- □ **boring** 形 うんざりさせる, 退屈な
- □ **Boshin** 名《War of –》戊辰戦争《慶応4年（1868）戊辰の年1月から翌年5月にかけて, 維新政府軍と旧幕府派との間で行われた内戦》
- □ **bow** 動 （〜に）お辞儀する
- □ **brainstorm** 動 ブレインストーミングを行う
- □ **brave** 形 勇敢な
- □ **break in** 力ずくで入り込む, 侵入する
- □ **break out** （戦争が）勃発する
- □ **bride** 名 花嫁, 新婦
- □ **briefly** 副 短く, 簡潔に
- □ **brilliant** 形 光り輝く, 見事な, すばらしい
- □ **bring back** 戻す, 呼び戻す
- □ **British** 形 ①英国人の ②イギリス英語の 名 英国人
- □ **broker** 動 仲介[調停]する
- □ **brutal** 形 残酷な
- □ **bullet** 名 銃弾
- □ **bureaucrat** 名 役人, 官僚主義的な人
- □ **bury** 動 埋葬する, 埋める
- □ **bush** 名 低木の茂み **beat around the bush** 遠回しに[回りくどい]言い方をする
- □ **but** 熟 not 〜 but … 〜ではなくて…

C

- □ **calculation** 名 計算, 予測, 推測
- □ **calendar** 名 カレンダー, 暦
- □ **call on** 呼びかける, 招集する, 求める

- □ **calm** 形 穏やかな, 落ち着いた **calm down** 静まる
- □ **camp** 動 野営する
- □ **campaign** 名 ①キャンペーン（活動, 運動）②政治運動, 選挙運動 ③軍事行動
- □ **can** 熟 as 〜 as one can できる限り〜
- □ **candle** 名 ろうそく
- □ **cane** 名 茎 sugar cane サトウキビ
- □ **capable** 形 ○《be – of 〜ing》〜の能力[資質]がある ②有能な
- □ **capital** 名 首都
- □ **care** 熟 care about 〜を気に掛ける take care of 〜の世話をする, 〜面倒を見る, 〜を管理する take good care of 〜を大事に扱う, 大切にする
- □ **career** 名 ①（生涯の・専門的な）職業 ②経歴, キャリア
- □ **carry out** [計画を]実行する
- □ **casual** 形 略式の, カジュアルな, おざなりの
- □ **catastrophic** 形 大惨事の, 破滅的な
- □ **cave** 名 洞穴, 洞窟
- □ **cease-fire** 名 休戦, 停戦
- □ **cell** 名 独房
- □ **central** 形 中央の, 主要な
- □ **centralized** 形 中央集権化の **centralized government** 中央集権国家
- □ **ceremony** 名 儀式, 式典 **unveiling ceremony** 除幕式
- □ **certainty** 名 確信, 確実性
- □ **cesspool** 名 汚水だめ
- □ **challenge** 動 挑む, 試す
- □ **chamber** 名 部屋, 室
- □ **Chancellor** 名 （オーストリア・ドイツの）首相
- □ **chaos** 名 無秩序, 混乱状態
- □ **chaotic** 形 大混乱の, 雑然とした, 混沌とした

95

- □ **charge** 名 ①責任 ②非難, 告発 **in charge of** ～を任せられて, ～を担当して, ～の責任を負って
- □ **chief** 形 最高位の, 第一の, 主要な
- □ **China** 名 中国《国名》
- □ **chore** 名 雑用, 雑役 **administrative chore** 管理業務
- □ **Chōshū** 名 長州藩
- □ **Christian** 名 キリスト教徒, クリスチャン 形 キリスト(教)の
- □ **Christianity** 名 キリスト教, キリスト教信仰
- □ **circumstance** 名 (周囲の)事情, 状況, 環境
- □ **civil** 形 ①一般人の, 民間(人)の ②国内の, 国家の **civil war** 内戦, 内乱 **the Civil War** (19世紀アメリカの)南北戦争
- □ **claim** 名 ①主張, 断言 ②要求, 請求
- □ **clan** 名 ①氏族 ②一家, 一門
- □ **clash** 動 (意見, 利害が)衝突する
- □ **clear** 形 はっきりした, 明白な
- □ **cleverness** 名 賢さ, 利口さ
- □ **climate** 名 気候
- □ **closely** 副 ①密接に ②念入りに, 詳しく ③ぴったりと
- □ **clung** 動 cling (くっつく)の過去, 過去分詞
- □ **collaboration** 名 協力, 協調
- □ **colleague** 名 同僚, 仲間, 同業者
- □ **come across** ～に出くわす, ～に遭遇する
- □ **come after** ～のあとを追う
- □ **come to a halt** 中断される
- □ **come up with** ～を思いつく, 考え出す, 見つけ出す
- □ **comfort** 動 心地よくする, ほっとさせる, 慰める
- □ **comfortable** 形 快適な, 心地いい
- □ **command** 動 命令する, 指揮する

- □ **commander** 名 司令官, 指揮官 **divisional commander** 師団長
- □ **commerce** 名 商業, 貿易
- □ **commit** 動 (罪などを)犯す **commit suicide** 自殺する
- □ **commodore** 名 海軍准将, 提督
- □ **common** 熟 **in common** 共通して
- □ **communication** 名 伝えること, 伝導, 連絡
- □ **compensation** 名 補償[賠償]金, 補償
- □ **complain** 動 不平[苦情]を言う
- □ **complaint** 名 不平, 不満
- □ **completely** 副 完全に, すっかり
- □ **complex** 形 入り組んだ, 複雑な 名 強迫観念 **inferiority complex** 劣等感
- □ **complexity** 名 錯雑, 複雑さ
- □ **complicated** 形 ①複雑な ②むずかしい, 困難な
- □ **compromise** 動 譲歩する, 妥協する **compromise on** ～に関して妥協する
- □ **comrade** 名 (通例男性の)仲間, 同僚, 同志
- □ **concentrate** 動 一点に集める[集まる], 集中させる[する]
- □ **concern** 名 ①関心事 ②関心, 心配 ③関係, 重要性
- □ **condemn** 動 責める
- □ **condition** 名 ①(健康)状態, 境遇 ②《-s》状況, 様子 ③条件
- □ **confine** 動 閉じ込める
- □ **conflict** 名 ①不一致, 衝突 ②争い, 対立 ③論争
- □ **confront** 動 ①直面する, 立ち向かう ②突き合わせる, 比較する
- □ **connect** 動 つながる, つなぐ, 関係づける
- □ **connection** 名 つながり, 関係
- □ **consequently** 副 したがって, 結果として

WORD LIST

□ **conservative** 形 保守的な

□ **consider** 動 ①考慮する、～しようと思う ②(～と)みなす ③気にかける、思いやる

□ **considerable** 形 相当な、かなりの、重要な

□ **conspiracy** 名 陰謀、共謀

□ **constitution** 名 憲法

□ **contrary** 形 逆 to the contrary それとは反対に

□ **contrast** 名 対照、対比 in contrast to ～と対照をなして

□ **contribution** 名 貢献

□ **control** 動 ①管理[支配]する ②抑制する、コントロールする 名 ①管理、支配(力) ②抑制

□ **controversy** 名 論争、議論

□ **conversation** 名 会話、会談

□ **convert** 動 変える、転換する、改宗させる

□ **cooperation** 名 協力、協業、協調

□ **coordinate** 動 ①調和的になる、同格になる ②調整する、協調させる

□ **corner** 動 窮地に追い込む、追い詰める

□ **cost** 動 (金・費用が)かかる、(～を)要する、(人に金額を)費やさせる

□ **could** 熟 How could ～? 何だって～なんてことがありようか? If +《主語》+ could ～できればなあ《仮定法》

□ **counterforce** 名 (敵の攻撃に対する)反撃能力

□ **countless** 形 無数の、数え切れない

□ **countryside** 名 地方、田舎

□ **court** 名 宮廷 imperial court 皇室

□ **cover** 動 覆う、包む

□ **create** 動 創造する、生み出す、引き起こす

□ **creation** 名 創造[物]

□ **cricket** 名 コオロギ

□ **crisis** 名 ①危機、難局 ②重大局面

□ **cruelty** 名 残酷さ、残酷な行為[言動・言葉]

□ **crush** 動 押しつぶす、砕く、粉々にする

□ **cry out** 叫ぶ

□ **cunning** 形 ずるい、狡猾な

□ **current** 形 現在の、目下の

D

□ **daily** 形 毎日の、日常の

□ **damage** 動 損害を与える、損なう

□ **dawn** 名 夜明け

□ **day** 熟 all day long 一日中、終日 in those days あのころは、当時は

□ **deal** 動《- with ～》～を扱う 名 (不特定の)量、額 a good [great] deal (of ～) かなり[ずいぶん・大量](の～)、多額(の～)

□ **death** 名 死、死ぬこと

□ **deceive** 動 だます、あざむく

□ **decision** 名 決定、決心

□ **declare** 動 宣言する

□ **decline** 動 ①断る ②傾く ③衰える

□ **deem** 動 (～であると)考える

□ **deeply** 副 深く、非常に

□ **defeat** 動 打ち破る、負かす 名 敗北

□ **delay** 動 遅らせる、延期する

□ **delegation** 名 代表団、派遣団

□ **deliberately** 副 故意に、意図的に

□ **delicate** 形 繊細な、壊れやすい

□ **demand** 動 ①要求する、尋ねる ②必要とする 名 ①要求、請求 ②需要

□ **denounce** 動 非難する、告発する

□ **department** 名 部門、課、局

police department 警察

□ **depend** 動《 – on [upon] ～》①～を頼る, ～をあてにする ②～による

□ **deployment** 名 (軍隊などの) 配置, 展開

□ **descend** 動下りる **descend into** (悪い状態に) 陥る

□ **desert** 動見捨てる

□ **despair** 動絶望する, あきらめる 名絶望

□ **desperate** 形 ①絶望的な, 見込みのない ②ほしくてたまらない, 必死の

□ **despise** 動～を見下す

□ **despite** 前～にもかかわらず

□ **destroy** 動破壊する, 絶滅させる

□ **deteriorate** 動 ①悪化 [低下・退廃] する ②悪化させる

□ **determine** 動 ①決心する [させる] ②決定する [させる]

□ **develop** 動 ①発達する [させる] ②開発する

□ **dictator** 名独裁者, 専制者

□ **die out** 絶滅する

□ **differently** 副 (～と) 異なって, 違って

□ **diminish** 動減らす, 減少する, 小さくする

□ **diplomacy** 名外交, 外交的手腕

□ **diplomatic** 形外交 (上) の, 外交官の

□ **direct** 動命令する, 指図する

□ **direction** 名方向, 方角 **in the direction of** ～の方向に

□ **directive** 名指示, 命令

□ **directly** 副 ①じかに ②まっすぐに ③ちょうど

□ **disappear** 動消える, 存在しなくなる

□ **disappoint** 動失望させる, がっかりさせる

□ **disappointment** 名失望

□ **discontent** 名不平, 不満

□ **discontented** 形不平 [不満] のある, 面白くない

□ **discussion** 名討議, 討論

□ **disguise** 名変装 (すること), 見せかけ

□ **dismay** 動ろうばいさせる

□ **dispatch** 動派遣する

□ **disrespectful** 形失礼な, 無礼な

□ **disruption** 名混乱

□ **distance** 名距離, 隔たり, 遠方

□ **distill** 動蒸留する

□ **divide** 動分かれる, 分ける, 割れる, 割る **divide into** ～に分かれる

□ **divine** 形神聖な, 神の

□ **divisional** 形師団の **divisional commander** 師団長

□ **do one's best** 全力を尽くす

□ **domain** 名領地, 領土, 藩

□ **domestic** 形国内の, 自国の

□ **dominate** 動支配する, 統治する

□ **doubt** 動疑う

□ **downfall** 名失墜, 失脚

□ **downtown** 名街の中心, 繁華街

□ **draft** 名徴兵

□ **drastic** 形強烈な, 徹底した

□ **draw** 動引く, 引っ張る **draw to an end** 終わりに近づく

□ **drawn** 動 draw (引く) の過去分詞

□ **drew** 動 draw (引く) の過去

□ **drinker** 名酒飲み **heavy drinker** 大酒飲み

□ **drive someone out** (人) を追い払う

□ **driven** 動 drive (追い立てる) の過去分詞

□ **drunk** 熟 **get drunk** 酔う, 酩酊する

□ **due to** ～によって, ～が原因で

□ **Dutch** 形オランダの 名オランダ人の

WORD LIST

E

- **easily** 副 ①容易に, たやすく, 苦もなく ②気楽に
- **eastern** 形 東方の, 東向きの
- **echo** 動 反響させる[する]
- **economic** 形 経済学の, 経済上の
- **economy** 名 ①経済, 財政 ②節約
- **edict** 名 布告, 政令
- **educate** 動 教育する, (～するように)訓練する
- **educated** 形 教養のある, 教育を受けた
- **education** 名 教育, 教養
- **effective** 形 効果的である, 有効である
- **efficient** 形 効率的な, 有効な
- **effort** 名 努力(の成果)
- **eke** 動 やりくりする, 補足する
- **eliminate** 動 削除[排除・除去]する, 撤廃する
- **else** 熟 no one else 他の誰一人として～しない
- **elsewhere** 副 どこかほかの所で[へ]
- **embrace** 動 (主義・思想などを)受け入れる
- **emotion** 名 感激, 感動, 感情
- **emotional** 形 感情的な, 感激しやすい
- **emperor** 名 天皇
- **employ** 動 (人を)雇う, 使う
- **employer** 名 雇主, 使用[利用]する人
- **enable** 動 (～することを)可能にする, 容易にする
- **encounter** 動 (思いがけなく)出会う, 遭う
- **encourage** 動 勇気づける
- **end** 熟 draw to an end 終わりに近づく in the end とうとう, 結局, ついに

- **endure** 動 我慢する, 耐え忍ぶ
- **enemy** 名 敵 enemy line 敵陣
- **engage in** 《be -》～に従事している
- **engagement** 名 《軍事》戦闘, 交戦
- **England** 名 ①イングランド ②英国
- **enthusiasm** 名 情熱, 熱意, 熱心
- **entire** 形 全体の, 完全な, まったくの
- **entirely** 副 完全に, まったく
- **entreaty** 名 懇願, 嘆願
- **entryway** 名 (建物への)通路
- **envoy** 名 使館, 使者, 外交使節
- **era** 名 時代, 年代
- **eruption** 名 噴火
- **espionage** 名 偵察, スパイ
- **establish** 動 確立する, 立証する, 設置[設立]する
- **Europe** 名 ヨーロッパ
- **even if** たとえ～でも
- **even though** ～であるけれども, ～にもかかわらず
- **even-more-distant** 形 更に遠く離れた
- **eventually** 副 結局は
- **everybody** 代 誰でも, 皆
- **everyone** 代 誰でも, 皆
- **everything** 代 すべてのこと[もの], 何でも, 何もかも
- **exceedingly** 副 はなはだしく, 非常に
- **executive** 形 実行の, 執行の
- **exert** 動 ①(力・知力・能力を)出す, 発揮する ②(権力を)行使する
- **exhaust** 動 ①ひどく疲れさせる ②使い果たす
- **exile** 名 追放(者), 亡命(者) 動 追放する
- **existing** 形 現存の, 現在の, 現行

の

□ **expand** 動広げる, 拡張[拡大]する

□ **expect** 動予期[予測]する, (当然のこととして)期待する

□ **expel** 動追い出す, 吐き出す, 駆逐する

□ **explode** 動爆発する[させる]

□ **express** 動表現する, 述べる

□ **extent** 名範囲, 程度, 広さ, 広がり

□ **eye-opening** 形目を見張るような, 驚くべき

F

□ **facilitate** 動容易にする, 促進する

□ **fact** 熟 in fact つまり, 実は, 要するに

□ **faction** 名党派, 派閥

□ **factor** 名要因, 要素, 因子

□ **fair** 形正しい, 公平[正当]な

□ **fake** 形にせの

□ **fall into** ～に陥る

□ **fanatic** 形狂信的な, 熱狂的な

□ **far away** 遠く離れて

□ **far too** あまりにも～過ぎる

□ **farm** 動耕作する

□ **farmer** 名農民, 農場経営者

□ **farther** 副もっと遠く, さらに先に

□ **fatal** 形致命的な

□ **fate** 名運命, 宿命

□ **fault** 名過失, 誤り at fault 責任のある

□ **favor** 熟 in favor of ～に賛成して, ～を支持して

□ **fear** 名①恐れ ②心配, 不安 with fear 怖がって 動①恐れる ②心配する

□ **feeling** 名感じ, 気持ち

□ **feudal** 形封建制度の, 封建的な

□ **fief** 名領地, 封土

□ **fierce** 形どう猛な, 荒々しい, すさまじい, 猛烈な

□ **fight back** 反撃に転じる, 応戦する

□ **fighting** 名戦闘

□ **figure** 名人物, 大立者 熟 figure out 理解する, ～であるとわかる, (原因などを)解明する

□ **final** 形最後の, 決定的な 名①最後のもの ②期末[最終]試験 ③《-s》決勝戦

□ **financial** 形財務(上)の, 金融(上)の

□ **financially** 副財政的に, 金銭的に

□ **first of all** まず第一に

□ **fit** 形適当な, 相応な a fit subject for ～に適したテーマ[話題]

□ **flame** 名炎

□ **fleet** 名艦隊, 船団

□ **flex** 動(筋肉を)ほぐす flex one's muscles 力[威力]を示す[誇示する]

□ **flood** 動①氾濫する, 氾濫させる ②殺到する

□ **follower** 名信奉者, 追随者

□ **following** 形《the –》次の, 次に続く

□ **force** 名部隊, 警察, 《- s》軍隊 動①強制する, 力ずくで～する, 余儀なく～させる ②押しやる, 押し込む

□ **foreigner** 名外国人

□ **foremost** 形真っ先の, 第一の

□ **forgave** 動 forgive (許す)の過去

□ **forgive** 動許す, 免除する

□ **form** 動形づくる

□ **formal** 形正式の, 公式の

□ **formally** 副正式に, 公式に

□ **former** 形①前の, 先の, 以前の ②《the –》(二者のうち)前者の

□ **forthcoming** 形来るべき, 今度の, 手近にある

WORD LIST

- **fortunately** 副 幸運にも
- **forward** 副 ①前方に ②将来に向けて ③先へ、進んで **look forward to** ～を期待する
- **foster** 動 育てる、促進させる
- **fracture** 動 砕ける、折れる、骨折する
- **frank** 形 率直な、隠し立てをしない
- **French** 形 フランス(人・語)の 名 ①フランス語 ②《the –》フランス人
- **friendly** 形 親しみのある、親切な、友情のこもった
- **friendship** 名 友人であること、友情
- **frozen** 動 freeze (凍る) の過去分詞
- **frustrate** 動 ①挫折させる ②いらいらさせる、欲求不満を起こさせる
- **frustrated** 形 挫折した、失望した
- **frustration** 名 欲求不満、失意、挫折
- **Fukuoka** 名 福岡の変《1877年(明治10)3月27日に発生した福岡藩士族による士族反乱》
- **fully** 副 十分に、完全に、まるまる
- **fundamentally** 副 根本的に
- **furious** 形 怒り狂った、激怒した、激しい
- **Fushimi** 名 伏見《京都の地名》

G

- **gain** 動 得る、増す
- **gaze** 動 凝視する
- **general** 名 大将、将軍
- **generation** 名 世代
- **genius** 名 天才、才能
- **German** 形 ドイツ(人・語)の 名 ①ドイツ人 ②ドイツ語
- **Germany** 名 ドイツ《国名》
- **Gesshō** 名 月照《幕末期の尊皇攘夷派の僧侶、1813–1858》
- **get** 熟 **get along** やっていく、はかどる **get along with** (人) と仲良くする、気[うま]が合う、歩調を合わせる **get back** 戻る、帰る **get drunk** 酔う、酩酊する **get going** ①急ぐ ②出かける、出発する **get rid of** ～を取り除く **get someone to do** (人) に～させる[してもらう] **get the better of** ～に勝つ **get to do** ～できるようになる、～できる機会を得る
- **give up** あきらめる、やめる、引き渡す
- **global** 形 地球(上)の、地球規模の、世界的な、国際的な
- **go down to** ～まで降りていく
- **go into hiding** 身を潜める
- **go on and on about** ～について延々と話す
- **go through** (困難・試練などを) 体験[経験]する
- **gotten** 動 get (得る) の過去分詞
- **govern** 動 治める、管理する、支配する **centralized government** 中央集権国家
- **government** 名 政治、政府、支配 **government administrator** 行政官
- **governmental** 形 政治の、行政機関の、政府の、国営の
- **governor** 名 支配者、長
- **gradually** 副 だんだんと
- **grant** 名 授与
- **grasp** 動 つかむ、握る、とらえる、理解する 名 把握、理解(力)
- **gravely** 副 重々に
- **great deal** 多量に、大いに
- **greatly** 副 大いに
- **grievance** 名 ①(労働条件に対する)不平 ②憤り
- **grow -er and -er** ますます～する
- **guilty** 形 罪の意識がある
- **guard** 名 番人

101

- □ **gun** 图銃, 大砲
- □ **gunfire** 图発砲

H

- □ **Hagi** 图萩の乱《1876年(明治9)に山口県萩で起こった, 明治政府に対する士族反乱》
- □ **hairstyle** 图ヘアスタイル, 髪型
- □ **halt** 图中止, 休止 **come to a halt** 中断される
- □ **Hamaguri Gate** 《Battle of ~》蛤御門の変《元治元年(1864)長州藩が京都に出兵し, 会津・薩摩などの藩兵と蛤御門付近で戦って敗れた事件》
- □ **han** 图藩
- □ **hand** 熟 **hand over** 手渡す, 引き渡す, 譲渡する **on the other hand** 一方, 他方では
- □ **handle** 動取り扱う
- □ **harm** 動傷つける
- □ **harmony** 图調和, 一致
- □ **harsh** 形厳しい, とげとげしい, 不快な
- □ **harshly** 副厳しく, 無情に
- □ **hate** 動嫌う, 憎む, (~するのを)いやがる
- □ **head of** ~の長
- □ **headquarters** 图本部, 司令部, 本署
- □ **heal** 動いえる, いやす, 治る, 治す
- □ **hear of** ~について聞く
- □ **heavy drinker** 大酒飲み
- □ **hegemony** 图覇権, 支配権
- □ **help in** ~に役立つ
- □ **hesitate** 動ためらう, ちゅうちょする
- □ **hid** 動 hide (隠れる)の過去, 過去分詞
- □ **hide** 動隠れる, 隠す, 隠れて見えない, 秘密にする **go into hiding** 身を潜める

- □ **high-rank** 形高位の, 地位の高い
- □ **high-ranking** 形高位の, 地位の高い
- □ **Hisamitsu** 图島津 久光《幕末・明治の政治家。幕末の薩摩藩における事実上の最高権力者, 1817–1887》
- □ **hoe** 動くわで掘る
- □ **home** 熟 **at home** 自宅で
- □ **homeland** 图母国, 祖国, 本土
- □ **homeless** 形家のない, ホームレスの
- □ **honor** 图①名誉, 光栄, 信用 ②節操, 自尊心
- □ **honorable** 形名誉ある **honorable death** 名誉の死
- □ **hostilities** 图交戦(状態), 戦闘
- □ **household** 图世帯
- □ **How could ~?** 何だって~なんてことがありえようか?
- □ **however** 副たとえ~でも 接けれども, だが
- □ **huge** 形巨大な, ばく大な
- □ **hull** 图船体
- □ **human being** 人, 人間
- □ **humid** 形湿った, むしむしする
- □ **hunting** 形狩猟の
- □ **husky** 形(体格の)がっちりした, 頑丈な

I

- □ **ideal** 图理想, 究極の目標
- □ **idealist** 图理想主義者, 夢想家, 観念論者
- □ **Iemochi** 图徳川 家茂《江戸幕府第14代征夷大将軍, 在職: 1858–1866》
- □ **Iesada** 图徳川 家定《江戸幕府第13代征夷大将軍, 在職: 1853–1858》
- □ **if** 熟 **If** + 《主語》 + **could** ~できればなあ《仮定法》 **as if** あたかも~のように, まるで~みたいに **even if** たとえ~でも **wonder if** ~ではないかと

102

WORD LIST

思う

- □ **ignore** 動 ～を無視する
- □ **Ii Naosuke** 井伊 直弼《幕末の譜代大名。近江彦根藩の第15代藩主。幕末期の江戸幕府にて大老。1815–1860》
- □ **Ikedaya Inn** 名 池田屋《京都三条木屋町 (三条小橋) の旅館》
- □ **illegal** 形 違法な、不法な
- □ **image** 名 印象、姿
- □ **imagine** 動 想像する、心に思い描く
- □ **immediate** 形 さっそくの、即座の、直接の
- □ **immediately** 副 すぐに、～するやいなや
- □ **immerse** 動 ①浸す、沈める ②没頭させる
- □ **imperial** 形 皇室の Imperial Army 官軍 Imperial Palace 皇居
- □ **impressed** 形 印象づけられて、感銘を受けて
- □ **impressive** 形 印象的な、深い感銘を与える
- □ **improve** 動 改善する [させる]、進歩する
- □ **incense** 名 香、芳香
- □ **incident** 名 出来事、事故、事変、紛争
- □ **including** 前 ～を含めて、込みで
- □ **indeed** 副 ①実際、本当に ②《強意》まったく 間 本当に、まさか
- □ **independence** 名 独立、自立
- □ **India** 名 インド《国名》
- □ **indirectly** 副 間接 (的) に、遠回しに
- □ **indispensable** 形 必要不可欠な、欠くことのできない
- □ **inferiority** 名 劣っていること、劣等 inferiority complex 劣等感
- □ **influence** 名 影響、勢力
- □ **influential** 形 影響力の大きい、有力な

- □ **infrastructure** 名 インフラ、(社会) 基盤、
- □ **infringe** 動 (権利・法律などを) 侵す、侵害する be infringed upon 侵害される
- □ **injure** 動 痛める、傷つける
- □ **inn** 名 宿屋、居酒屋
- □ **innate** 形 生まれつきの、先天的な、内在的な
- □ **insect** 名 虫、昆虫
- □ **insist** 動 ①主張する、断言する ②要求する
- □ **install** 動 据えつける、設置する
- □ **instant** 名 瞬間、寸時 in an instant たちまち、ただちに
- □ **instead** 副 その代わりに instead of ～の代わりに、～をしないで
- □ **institute** 動 制定する
- □ **insult** 動 侮辱する、ばかにする
- □ **integrate** 動 ①統合する、一体化する ②溶け込ませる、溶け込む、差別をなくす
- □ **intellectual** 名 知識人、有識者
- □ **intend** 動《– to ～》～しようと思う、～するつもりである
- □ **intense** 形 強烈な、激しい
- □ **intention** 名 ①意図、(～する) つもり ②心構え
- □ **interested** 動 be interested in ～に興味 [関心] がある
- □ **interesting** 形 おもしろい、興味を起こさせる
- □ **international affairs** 国際情勢
- □ **invade** 動 侵入する、攻め入る
- □ **invader** 名 侵入者、侵略国、侵略軍
- □ **involve** 動 ①含む、伴う ②巻き込む、かかわらせる
- □ **ironic** 形 皮肉な、反語的な
- □ **islander** 名 島民
- □ **isolate** 動 隔離する、孤立させる
- □ **isolated** 形 隔離した、孤立した

SAIGŌ TAKAMORI

□ **issue** 图問題, 論点

□ **It is ~ for someone to ...** (人)が…するのは〜だ

□ **Itō Hirobumi** 伊藤 博文《日本の武士（長州藩士）, 政治家, 1841–1909》

□ **Itoko** 图西郷 糸子《西郷隆盛の3度目の妻, 1843–1922》

□ **itself** 代それ自体, それ自身

□ **Iwakura Tomomi** 岩倉 具視《日本の公家, 政治家, 1825–1883》

J

□ **Japan** 图日本《国名》

□ **Japanese** 形日本（人・語）の 图①日本人 ②日本語

□ **judicial** 形裁判（官）の, 司法の

□ **judiciary** 图司法（制度）

K

□ **Katsu Kaishū** 勝 海舟《幕末から明治時代初期の武士（幕臣）, 政治家, 1823–1899》

□ **Kazuno-miya** 图和宮 親子内親王《仁孝天皇の第八皇女, 江戸幕府第14代将軍徳川家茂の正室, 1846–1877》

□ **keen** 形①鋭い, 鋭敏な ②熱心な

□ **keep track of** 〜の経過を追う, 〜の記録をつける

□ **Kido Kōin** 木戸 孝允（桂 小五郎）《日本の武士（長州藩士）, 政治家, 1833–1877》

□ **Kikujirō** 图西郷 菊次郎《日本の政治家, 外交官。西郷隆盛と愛子（愛加那）の長子, 1861–1928》

□ **killer** 图殺人者［犯］

□ **kind of** 〜のようなもの

□ **kindly** 副親切に, 優しく

□ **kingdom** 图王国

□ **Kirino** 图桐野 利秋《日本の武士（薩摩藩士）, 陸軍軍人, 1838–1877》

□ **knowledge** 图知識, 理解, 学問

□ **known as** 熟《be 〜》〜として知られている

□ **Kōmei** 图孝明天皇《第121代天皇, 在位：弘化3年2月13日（1846年3月10日）–慶応2年12月25日（1867年1月30日）》

□ **Korea** 图朝鮮, 韓国《国名》

□ **Korean** 形韓国（人・語）の, 朝鮮（人・語）の 图①韓国［朝鮮］人 ②韓国［朝鮮］語 **Korean Issue** 対朝鮮問題

□ **Kumamoto** 图神風連の乱《1876年（明治9）に熊本市で起こった, 明治政府に対する士族反乱》

□ **Kuwana** 图桑名藩

L

□ **launch** 動（事業などを）始める

□ **lay** 動lie（〜のままでいる, 埋葬されて［葬られて］いる）の過去

□ **lead to** 〜に至る, 〜に通じる, 〜を引き起こす

□ **leadership** 图指揮, リーダーシップ

□ **leading** 形主要な, 指導的な, 先頭の

□ **least** 副いちばん小さく, 最も少なく 图最小, 最少 **at least** 少なくとも

□ **leave over** 残しておく

□ **leave ~ for ...** …を〜のために残しておく

□ **led** 動lead（導く）の過去, 過去分詞

□ **legislative** 形立法上の, 立法機関の

□ **less** 形〜より小さい［少ない］ 副〜より少なく, 〜ほどでなく

□ **let down** 期待を裏切る, 失望させる

104

WORD LIST

- [ ] **lie** 動①うそを言う ②存在する, ～のままでいる, 埋葬されて[葬られて]いる
- [ ] **lieutenant general** 中将
- [ ] **like** 熟 look like ～のように見える
- [ ] **likeness** 名 (～に)よく似ていること
- [ ] **link** 動連結する, つながる
- [ ] **lip** 名唇, 《-s》口
- [ ] **locate** 動置く, 居住する[させる]
- [ ] **London** 名ロンドン《英国の首都》
- [ ] **lonely** 形①孤独な, 心さびしい ②ひっそりした, 人里離れた
- [ ] **long** 熟 all day long 一日中, 終日
- [ ] **long-time** 形長年の, 長期にわたる
- [ ] **look for** ～を探す
- [ ] **look forward to** ～を期待する
- [ ] **look like** ～のように見える
- [ ] **look on** ～を見る[見詰める]
- [ ] **lookout** 名①見張り, 警戒 ②見込み
- [ ] **loom** 動ぼんやりと現れる, 巨大な姿を現す loom over ～にぼんやり現れる
- [ ] **loop** 名ループ, 輪, 輪状のもの out of the loop 蚊帳の外に置かれて, 中枢から外れて
- [ ] **lop** 動切り取る, 切り落とす lop ～ off with …で～を切り落とす
- [ ] **lord** 名領主, 藩主
- [ ] **lose** 熟 have any time to lose ぐずぐずしている時間がない, 一刻を争う
- [ ] **loser** 名敗者
- [ ] **loss** 名①損失(額・物), 損害, 浪費 ②失敗, 敗北
- [ ] **loudly** 副大声で, 騒がしく
- [ ] **lower** 形もっと低い, 下級の, 劣った
- [ ] **lowlife** 名ごろつき, ならず者
- [ ] **loyal** 形忠実な, 誠実な

- [ ] **loyalist** 名愛国者, 忠臣, 政府支持者

M

- [ ] **magnificent** 形壮大な, 壮麗な, すばらしい
- [ ] **main** 形主な, 主要な
- [ ] **mainland** 名本土, 大陸
- [ ] **mainly** 副主に
- [ ] **maintain** 動維持する
- [ ] **major** 形大きいほうの, 主な
- [ ] **manage** 動①動かす, うまく処理する ②経営[管理]する, 支配する ③どうにか～する
- [ ] **Manchuria** 名満州《地名》
- [ ] **manipulate** 動操る, 操作する, 巧みに扱う
- [ ] **mark** 熟 make one's mark 有名になる, 名を成す[上げる], 出世する 動①印[記号]をつける ②目立たせる
- [ ] **marriage** 名結婚
- [ ] **marry** 動結婚する
- [ ] **master** 名主人, 雇い主, 師
- [ ] **material** 形物質の, 肉体的な
- [ ] **matter-of-fact** 形事実に即した, 率直な
- [ ] **mediation** 名調停, 仲介
- [ ] **meeting** 名集まり, ミーティング
- [ ] **Meiji** 名明治(時代)《1868–1912》 Emperor Meiji 明治天皇 Meiji era 明治時代 Meiji Restoration 明治維新
- [ ] **memory** 名記憶(力), 思い出
- [ ] **mental** 形①心の, 精神の ②知能[知性]の
- [ ] **mention** 動 (～について)述べる, 言及する
- [ ] **merchant** 名商人, 貿易商
- [ ] **merciless** 形無慈悲な

105

- [ ] **middle** 名中間, 最中
- [ ] **might** 助《mayの過去》①~かもしれない ②~してもよい, ~できる
- [ ] **mile** 名①マイル《長さの単位。1,609m》②《-s》かなりの距離
- [ ] **military** 形軍隊[軍人]の, 軍事の 名《the－》軍, 軍部
- [ ] **mind** 名①心, 精神, 考え ②知性
- [ ] **mindful** 形心にかける, 注意して
- [ ] **minister** 名大臣, 閣僚, 公使
- [ ] **miserable** 形みじめな, 哀れな
- [ ] **mission** 名①使命, 任務 ②使節団, 代表団, 派遣団
- [ ] **mist** 名霧, もや
- [ ] **mistreatment** 名虐待, 酷使
- [ ] **misunderstanding** 名考え違い, 誤解
- [ ] **model** 名①模型, 設計図 ②模範
- [ ] **moderate** 形穏やかな, 適度な, 手ごろな
- [ ] **modern** 形現代[近代]の, 現代的な, 最近の
- [ ] **modernize** 動現代的になる, 近代化する
- [ ] **modest** 形謙虚な, 腰の低い
- [ ] **moment** 名①瞬間, ちょっとの間 ②(特定の)時, 時期
- [ ] **monitor** 動監視する, 観察する
- [ ] **monk** 名修道士, 僧
- [ ] **mount** 動(馬に)乗る, のせる
- [ ] **move on** 先に進む
- [ ] **moved** 熟《be－》感激する, 感銘する
- [ ] **movement** 名①動き, 運動 ②《-s》行動 ③引っ越し ④変動
- [ ] **much** 熟as much as ~と同じだけ
- [ ] **Mukden** 名(満州の)奉天《地名》
- [ ] **mumble** 動ぶつぶつ言う, つぶやく
- [ ] **muscle** 名筋肉, 腕力 flex one's muscles 力[威力]を示す[誇示する]

N

- [ ] **Nagaoka domain** 長岡藩
- [ ] **Nariakira** 名島津 斉彬《江戸時代後期から幕末の外様大名で, 薩摩藩の第11代藩主。島津氏第28代当主, 1809–1858》
- [ ] **nation** 名国, 国家, 《the－》国民
- [ ] **nationalism** 名ナショナリズム, 国家主義
- [ ] **native** 名(ある土地に)生まれた人
- [ ] **navy** 名海軍, 海軍力
- [ ] **necessary** 形必要な, 必然の
- [ ] **necessity** 名必要, 不可欠, 必要品
- [ ] **negotiate** 動交渉[協議]する
- [ ] **negotiation** 名交渉, 話し合い
- [ ] **neither** 副《否定文に続いて》~も…しない neither ~ nor … ~も…もない
- [ ] **network** 名網状組織, ネットワーク
- [ ] **newly** 副再び, 最近, 新たに
- [ ] **news** 名報道, ニュース, 便り, 知らせ
- [ ] **no** 熟in no time すぐに, 一瞬で no one 誰も[一人も] ~ない no one else 他の誰一人として~しない
- [ ] **nobility** 名①高貴さ ②《the－》貴族
- [ ] **nobody** 代誰も[1人も] ~ない
- [ ] **nod** 動うなずく
- [ ] **none** 代(~の)何も[誰も・少しも] …ない
- [ ] **nor** 接~もまたない neither ~ nor … ~も…もない
- [ ] **normal** 形普通の, 平均の, 標準的な
- [ ] **northern** 形北の, 北向きの, 北からの
- [ ] **nostalgic** 形懐かしい, 郷愁に満ちた, ノスタルジックな
- [ ] **not** 熟not up to the task 役割を果たせない not yet まだ~してな

WORD LIST

い **not ～ at all** 少しも［全然］～ない　**not ～ but …** ～ではなくて…　**whether or not** ～かどうか

O

☐ **obey** 動服従する，（命令などに）従う

☐ **observe** 動観察［観測］する，監視［注視］する

☐ **obstacle** 名障害(物)，じゃま(な物)

☐ **obtain** 動得る，獲得する

☐ **occupy** 動①占領する，保有する ②（職に）つく，従事する

☐ **offer** 動申し出る，申し込む，提供する

☐ **officer** 名役人，公務員，警察官　**police officer** 警察官

☐ **officially** 副公式に，職務上，正式に

☐ **Okino-Erabu island** 沖永良部島

☐ **Ōkubo Toshimichi** 大久保利通《日本の武士（薩摩藩士），政治家，1830–1878》

☐ **once** 熟**at once** すぐに，同時に

☐ **one and all** すべての人

☐ **one-sidedly** 副一方的に

☐ **openly** 副率直に，公然と

☐ **operate** 動活動する

☐ **operation** 名作戦，軍事行動

☐ **opportunity** 名好機，適当な時期［状況］

☐ **oppose** 動反対する，敵対する

☐ **order** 熟**in order to** ～するために，～しようと

☐ **organization** 名組織，団体，機関

☐ **organize** 動組織する

☐ **originally** 副元は，元来

☐ **other** 熟**in other words** すなわち，言い換えれば **on the other hand**

一方，他方では

☐ **out** 形《be ～》外出している

☐ **out of** ①～から外へ，～から抜け出して ②～から作り出して，～を材料として ③～の範囲外に，～から離れて ④（ある数）の中から **out of the loop** 蚊帳の外に置かれて，中枢から外れて

☐ **outcome** 名結果，結末

☐ **outright** 副完全に，徹底的に

☐ **outset** 名《the –》始め，最初

☐ **over** 形《be ～》終わる

☐ **overseas** 形海外の，外国の 副海外へ 名国外

☐ **overthrew** 動overthrow（ひっくり返す）の過去

☐ **overthrow** 動①ひっくり返す ②転覆する，廃止する

☐ **owe** 動①（～を）負う，（～を人の）お陰とする ②（金を）借りている，（人に対して～の）義務がある

☐ **Ōyama Iwao** 大山巌《日本の武士（薩摩藩士），陸軍軍人，政治家，1842–1916》

P

☐ **painful** 形①痛い，苦しい，痛ましい ②骨の折れる，困難な

☐ **palace** 名宮殿，大邸宅

☐ **panic** 動恐慌を引き起こす，うろたえる

☐ **parade** 名パレード，行列

☐ **parley** 交渉する，和平会談をする

☐ **particularly** 副特に，とりわけ

☐ **partner** 名仲間，同僚

☐ **pass away** 死ぬ

☐ **passion** 名情熱，（～への）熱中，激怒

☐ **past** 名過去（の出来事）

☐ **path** 名進路，通路

☐ **pathetic** 形哀れな，感傷的な

107

SAIGŌ TAKAMORI

- **patriot** 名 愛国者, 憂国の士
- **pay** 動 支払う, 払う, 報いる, 償う
  pay back 返済する, お返しをする
- **peaceful** 形 平和な, 穏やかな
- **penetrate** 動 ①貫く, 浸透する ②見抜く
- **penetrating** 形 突き刺すような
- **perhaps** 副 たぶん, ことによると
- **perilous** 形 危険な
- **period** 名 期, 期間, 時代
- **permission** 名 許可, 免許
- **Perry** 名《Commodore –》ペリー提督《マシュー・カルブレイス・ペリー (Matthew Calbraith Perry) アメリカ海軍の軍人, 1794–1858》
- **persistent** 形 ①しつこい, 頑固な ②持続する, 永続的な
- **personal** 形 ①個人の, 私的な ②本人自らの
- **personally** 副 個人的には, 自分で
- **persuade** 動 説得する, 促して〜させる
- **petition** 名 請願（書）, 嘆願
- **philosophy** 名 哲学, 主義, 信条, 人生観
- **piercing** 形 ①鋭い, 刺すような ②洞察力のある
- **pitch** 名 ピッチ《コールタールなどを蒸留した後に残る黒褐色の粘質物》
- **place** 熟 **take place** 行われる, 起こる
- **pleasantry** 名 社交辞令
- **pledge** 名 誓約, 約束
- **plow** 動 すく, 耕す
- **point of view** 考え方, 視点
- **police department** 警察
- **police officer** 警察官
- **policy** 名 政策, 方針
- **political** 形 政治の
- **politician** 名 政治家, 政略家
- **politics** 名 政治（学）, 政策

- **pool** 動 共同出資する
- **port** 名 港, 港町
- **position** 名 ①位置, 場所, 姿勢 ②地位, 身分, 職 ③立場, 状況
- **possible** 形 ①可能な ②ありうる, 起こりうる **as 〜 as possible** できるだけ〜
- **posture** 名 ①姿勢 ②（気取った）態度 ③状況
- **powerful** 形 力強い, 実力のある, 影響力のある
- **prefecture** 名 県, 府
- **prefer** 動 （〜のほうを）好む, （〜のほうが）よいと思う
- **presence** 名 存在すること
- **president** 名 大統領
- **pressing** 形 差し迫った, 緊急の
- **pressure** 名 プレッシャー, 圧力, 圧縮, 重荷
- **pretend** 動 ①ふりをする, 装う ②あえて〜しようとする
- **pride** 名 誇り, 自慢, 自尊心
- **prime minister** 首相, 内閣総理大臣
- **princess** 名 王女
- **prison** 名 刑務所, 監獄
- **prisoner** 名 囚人, 捕虜
- **private** 形 ①私的な, 個人の ②民間の, 私立の
- **privilege** 名 特権
- **pro-** 頭 〜賛成の, 〜支持の
- **procession** 名 行進, 行列
- **proclaim** 動 宣言［布告］する
- **professional** 形 専門の, プロの, 職業的な
- **progress** 名 進歩, 前進
- **prohibit** 動 禁止する, 差し止める
- **promote** 動 昇進［昇級］させる
- **promotion** 名 昇進
- **proposal** 名 提案, 計画
- **prosecute** 動 起訴する, 告訴する

WORD LIST

- [ ] **prosecution** 名 起訴, 求刑
- [ ] **proud** 形 自慢の, 誇った, 自尊心の ある **be proud of** ～を自慢に思う
- [ ] **provide** 動 供給する, 用意する
- [ ] **province** 名 州, 省, 県
- [ ] **provisional** 形 暫定的な, 仮の
- [ ] **prudent** 形 分別のある, 慎重な
- [ ] **public** 名 一般の人々, 大衆 **in public** 人前で, 公然と
- [ ] **punish** 動 罰する, ひどい目にあわせる
- [ ] **purchase** 動 購入する
- [ ] **purge** 動 粛清する, 一掃する, 追放する
- [ ] **pursue** 動 ①追う, つきまとう ②追求する, 従事する
- [ ] **push back** 押し返す, 押しのける
- [ ] **put on** ～を身につける, 着る
- [ ] **put out** 外に出す
- [ ] **put ～ into ...** ～を…の状態にする, ～を…に突っ込む

Q

- [ ] **quality** 名 ①質, 性質, 品質 ②特性 ③良質
- [ ] **quickly** 副 敏速に, 急いで
- [ ] **quietly** 副 ①静かに ②平穏に, 控えめに

R

- [ ] **radical** 形 急進的な, 過激な
- [ ] **raid** 動 急襲する
- [ ] **raise** 動 ～を育てる
- [ ] **rank** 名 階級, 位
- [ ] **rather** 副 かなり, いくぶん, やや
- [ ] **react** 動 反応する, 対処する
- [ ] **reaction** 名 反応, 反動, 反抗, 影響

- [ ] **reality** 名 現実, 実在, 真実(性)
- [ ] **reason** 熟 **for some reason** なんらかの理由で, どういうわけか
- [ ] **rebel** 名 反逆者, 反抗者 **rebel army** 反乱軍
- [ ] **rebellion** 名 反乱, 反抗, 謀反, 暴動
- [ ] **rebellious** 形 反抗的な, 反逆する, 反体制の
- [ ] **rebuff** 動 拒絶する
- [ ] **rebuild** 動 再建する, 改造する
- [ ] **recall** 動 思い出す, 思い出させる
- [ ] **recent** 形 近ごろの, 近代の
- [ ] **recently** 副 近ごろ, 最近
- [ ] **reckless** 形 無謀な, 見境のない
- [ ] **recognize** 動 認める, 認識[承認]する
- [ ] **recover** 動 ①取り戻す, ばん回する ②回復する
- [ ] **recruit** 動 (人材を)募集する, 勧誘する
- [ ] **reduce** 動 ①減じる ②しいて～させる, (～の)状態にする **be reduced to ashes** 焼けて灰になる
- [ ] **reform** 動 改善する, 改革する 名 改善, 改良
- [ ] **reformation** 名 矯正, 改心, 改良, 改善
- [ ] **reformer** 名 改革論者
- [ ] **refuse** 動 拒絶する, 断る
- [ ] **regain** 動 取り戻す, (～に)戻る
- [ ] **region** 名 ①地方, 地域 ②範囲
- [ ] **regret** 動 後悔する, 残念ながら～する 名 遺憾, 後悔, (～に対する)悲しみ
- [ ] **reject** 動 拒絶する, 断る
- [ ] **relation** 名 (利害)関係, 間柄
- [ ] **relationship** 名 関係, 関連
- [ ] **release** 動 解き放す, 釈放する 名 解放, 釈放
- [ ] **relieve** 動 (心配・苦痛などを)軽減する, ほっとさせる

- [ ] **relinquish** 動放棄する, 手放す
- [ ] **reluctant** 形気乗りしない, しぶしぶの
- [ ] **reluctantly** 副いやいやながら, 仕方なく
- [ ] **remain** 動①残っている, 残る ②(〜の)ままである[いる]
- [ ] **remaining** 形残った, 残りの
- [ ] **remote** 形①(距離・時間的に)遠い, 遠隔の ②人里離れた
- [ ] **rename** 動新しい名前をつける, 改名する
- [ ] **repair** 動修理[修繕]する 名修理, 修繕
- [ ] **repercussion** 名反響, 影響
- [ ] **reply** 動答える, 返事をする, 応答する 名答え, 返事, 応答
- [ ] **reputation** 名評判, 名声, 世評
- [ ] **require** 動①必要とする, 要する ②命じる, 請求する
- [ ] **rescind** 動廃止する, 破棄する
- [ ] **residence** 名住宅, 居住 **take up residence in** 〜に居を構える
- [ ] **resign** 動辞職する, やめる, 断念する
- [ ] **resignation** 名辞任
- [ ] **resist** 動抵抗[反抗・反撃]する, 耐える
- [ ] **resistance** 名抵抗, 反抗, 敵対
- [ ] **resolute** 形決心の固い, 断固たる
- [ ] **respect** 名①尊敬, 尊重 ②注意, 考慮 動尊敬[尊重]する
- [ ] **respective** 形それぞれの, 個別の
- [ ] **respond** 動答える, 返答[応答]する
- [ ] **response** 名応答, 反応, 返答
- [ ] **responsibility** 名責任, 義務, 義理
- [ ] **rest** 動休む
- [ ] **Restoration** 名《the－》王政復古 **Meiji Restoration** 明治維新
- [ ] **restore** 動元に戻す, 復活させる

- [ ] **result** 名結果, 成り行き **as a result** その結果(として)
- [ ] **retain** 動保つ, 持ち続ける
- [ ] **retaliation** 名仕返し, 報復
- [ ] **retire** 動退職[引退]する
- [ ] **retreat** 動後退する, 退く
- [ ] **reunite** 動再結合する, 再会させる
- [ ] **revenge** 名復讐
- [ ] **revenue** 名所得, 収入, 利益, (国の)歳入
- [ ] **reverence** 名尊敬, 崇拝
- [ ] **revive** 動生き返る, 生き返らせる, 復活する[させる]
- [ ] **revolving** 形回転する, 回転式の
- [ ] **reward** 動報いる, 報酬を与える
- [ ] **rid** 動取り除く **get rid of** 〜を取り除く
- [ ] **right** 熟**all right** 大丈夫で
- [ ] **risen** 動rise (昇る)の過去分詞
- [ ] **risk** 名危険
- [ ] **ritual** 名儀式
- [ ] **rival** 名競争相手, 匹敵する人
- [ ] **role** 名①(劇などの)役 ②役割, 任務
- [ ] **route** 名道, 道筋, 進路
- [ ] **ruin** 名破滅, 滅亡, 破産, 廃墟 **in ruins** 荒廃して 動破滅させる
- [ ] **rule over** 治める, 統御する
- [ ] **ruler** 名支配者
- [ ] **run up to** 〜に走り寄る
- [ ] **Russia** 名ロシア《国名》
- [ ] **Russian** 名ロシア(人・語)の 名①ロシア人 ②ロシア語
- [ ] **Russo-Japanese war** 日露戦争《日本とロシアの戦争, 1904–05》
- [ ] **Ryūkyū Kingdom** 琉球王国《1429年から1879年の間, 琉球諸島を中心に存在した王国》

WORD LIST

S

□ **sabotage** 動 ～に破壊［妨害］工作を行う

□ **saddened** 形 悲しむ, 悲しみに包まれた

□ **Saga** 名 佐賀の乱《1874年（明治7年）2月に江藤新平・島義勇らをリーダーとして佐賀で起こった, 明治政府に対する士族反乱》

□ **Saigō Kichinosuke** 西郷 吉之介《西郷隆盛の通称》

□ **Saigō Takamori** 西郷 隆盛《日本の武士（薩摩藩士）・軍人・政治家, 1828–1877》

□ **Saigō Tsugumichi** 西郷 従道《日本の武士（薩摩藩士）, 陸軍および海軍軍人, 政治家。西郷隆盛の弟, 1843–1902》

□ **sail** 動 帆走する, 航海する, 出航する

□ **Saitō Hajime** 斎藤 一《日本の武士（新撰組隊士）, 警察官, 1844–1915》

□ **sake** 名 （～の）ため, 利益, 目的

□ **samurai** 名 侍

□ **Satsuma** 名 薩摩藩

□ **scholar** 名 学者

□ **seclusion** 名 隔絶すること, 鎖国

□ **secondly** 副 第2に, 次に

□ **secret** 形 ①秘密の, 隠れた ②神秘の, 不思議な

□ **secretly** 副 秘密に, 内緒で

□ **secure** 動 ～を確保する

□ **seem** 動 （～に）見える, （～のように）思われる

□ **Seinan** 名《War of –》西南戦争《西郷隆盛を盟主にして起こった士族による武力反乱, 1877年》

□ **senior** 形 年長の, 年上の, 古参の, 上級の

□ **sense** 動 感じる, 気づく

□ **sentiment** 名 気持ち, 感情, 感傷

□ **seppuku** 名 切腹

□ **series** 名 一続き, 連続, シリーズ

□ **serious** 形 ①まじめな, 真剣な ②重大な, 深刻な, （病気などが）重い

□ **seriously** 副 ①真剣に, まじめに ②重大に

□ **servant** 名 召使, 使用人, しもべ

□ **serve** 動 仕える, 奉仕する

□ **set off on** （旅・航海など）に出発する

□ **set up** 配置する, セットする, 据え付ける, 設置する

□ **severe** 形 厳しい, 深刻な, 激しい

□ **severely** 副 鋭しく, 簡素に

□ **shameful** 形 恥ずべき, 下品な

□ **shape** 動 形づくる, 具体化する

□ **Shimazu Hisamatsu** 島津 久光《幕末・明治の政治家。幕末の薩摩藩における事実上の最高権力者, 1817–1887》

□ **Shimazu Nariakira** 島津 斉彬《江戸時代後期から幕末の外様大名で, 薩摩藩の第11代藩主。島津氏第28代当主, 1809–1858》

□ **Shinsen-gumi** 名 新撰組

□ **Shiroyama mountain** 城山

□ **shogun** 名 将軍

□ **shogunate** 名 将軍の職［政治］

□ **Shōka-Son Juku** 松下村塾《江戸時代末期に, 長州萩城下の松本村（現在の山口県萩市）に存在した私塾》

□ **shore** 名 岸, 海岸, 陸

□ **shoulder** 名 肩

□ **show off** 見せびらかす, 目立とうとする

□ **shut** 動 ①閉まる, 閉める, 閉じる ②shutの過去, 過去分詞

□ **side** 名 側

□ **silence** 名 沈黙, 無言, 静寂

□ **similar** 形 同じような, 類似した, 相似の

□ **simply** 副 ①簡単に ②単に, ただ ③まったく, 完全に

- □ **sincere** 形 誠実な, まじめな
- □ **sincerely** 副 真心をこめて
- □ **situation** 名 ①場所, 位置 ②状況, 境遇, 立場
- □ **skeptical** 形 懐疑的な, 疑い深い
- □ **skilled** 形 熟練した, 腕のいい, 熟練を要する
- □ **slam into** ~にぶつかる, 激突する
- □ **smart** 形 利口な, 抜け目のない
- □ **smooth** 動 滑らかにする, 平らにする **smooth things over** 事を丸く収める
- □ **so** 熟 **and so** そこで, それだから, それで **so that** ~するために, それで, ~できるように **so ~ that** … 非常に~なので…
- □ **So-called** 形 いわゆる
- □ **sob** 動 むせび泣く, 泣きじゃくる
- □ **social** 形 ①社会の, 社会的な ②社交的な, 愛想のよい
- □ **society** 名 社会, 世間
- □ **soldier** 名 兵士, 兵卒 動 軍人になる, 兵役につく
- □ **solution** 名 解決, 解明, 回答
- □ **solve** 動 解く, 解決する
- □ **some reason** 《for ~》なんらかの理由で, どういうわけか
- □ **somebody** 代 誰か, ある人
- □ **someday** 副 いつか, そのうち
- □ **somehow** 副 どうにかして
- □ **someone** 代 ある人, 誰か
- □ **something** 代 ①ある物, 何か ②いくぶん, 多少
- □ **sometimes** 副 時々, 時たま
- □ **soon** 熟 **as soon as** ~するとすぐ, ~するや否や
- □ **soul** 名 ①魂 ②精神, 心
- □ **soundly** 副 （敗北などが）完全に, すっかり
- □ **southern** 形 南の, 南向きの, 南からの
- □ **southwestern** 名 南西（部） 形 南西の, 南西向きの
- □ **sovereign** 形 独立した
- □ **spare** 動 ~なしですます, 容赦する
- □ **spirit** 名 精神, 気力
- □ **split** 動 裂く, 裂ける, 割る, 割れる, 分裂させる［する］
- □ **stare** 名 じっと見ること, 凝視
- □ **state** 名 国家 動 述べる, 表明する
- □ **statue** 名 像
- □ **status** 名 ①（社会的な）地位, 身分, 立場 ②状態
- □ **stay away from** ~から離れている
- □ **stay in** （場所）に泊まる, 滞在する
- □ **stay on** 居残る, とどまる
- □ **steam-powered** 蒸気駆動の
- □ **steamship** 名 汽船, 蒸気船
- □ **stifle** 動 ①窒息させる, 息の根を止める ②鎮圧する
- □ **stop by** 途中で立ち寄る, ちょっと訪ねる
- □ **storm** 名 嵐, 暴風雨
- □ **straightforward** 形 まっすぐな, 正直な, 率直な
- □ **strategy** 名 戦略, 作戦, 方針
- □ **strength** 名 長所, 強み
- □ **strictly** 副 厳しく, 厳密に
- □ **strongly** 副 強く, 頑丈に, 猛烈に, 熱心に
- □ **structure** 名 構造, 仕組み
- □ **struggle** 名 もがき, 奮闘
- □ **stuck** 動 stick（刺さる）の過去, 過去分詞
- □ **stupid** 形 ばかな, おもしろくない
- □ **style** 名 やり方, 流儀, 様式, スタイル
- □ **subordinate** 名 部下
- □ **suburb** 名 近郊, 郊外
- □ **succeed** 動 （~の）跡を継ぐ

WORD LIST

- □ **success** 名 成功, 幸運, 上首尾
- □ **successful** 形 成功した, うまくいった
- □ **successfully** 副 首尾よく, うまく
- □ **succession** 名 連続, 相続, 継承
- □ **successor** 名 後継者, 相続人, 後任者
- □ **such a** そのような, それほどの
- □ **suffer** 動 ①(苦痛・損害などを)受ける, こうむる ②(病気に)なる, 苦しむ, 悩む
- □ **sugar cane** サトウキビ
- □ **suicide** 名 自殺 **commit suicide** 自殺する
- □ **sumo wrestling** 相撲
- □ **superiority** 名 優勢, 優越, 優位(性)
- □ **superpower** 名 超大国, 強国, 異常な力
- □ **support** 動 支える, 支持する 名 支え, 支持
- □ **supporter** 名 後援者, 支持者, サポーター, 支柱
- □ **suppress** 動 抑える, 抑圧する
- □ **supreme** 形 最高の, 究極の
- □ **surplus** 名 余り, 残り, 余分, 余剰
- □ **surprise** 熟 **to one's surprise** 〜が驚いたことに
- □ **surprised** 動 surprise (驚かす) の過去, 過去分詞 形 驚いた
- □ **surrender** 動 降伏する, 引き渡す
- □ **surround** 動 囲む, 包囲する
- □ **surroundings** 名 周囲の状況, 環境
- □ **survive** 動 生き残る, 存続する, なんとかなる, 切り抜ける
- □ **survivor** 名 生存者, 残ったもの, 遺物
- □ **suspect** 動 疑う, (〜ではないかと)思う
- □ **suspicious** 形 あやしい, 疑い深い

- □ **swear** 動 ①誓う, 断言する ②口汚くののしる
- □ **sweet potato** さつまいも
- □ **swept** 動 sweep (掃く) の過去, 過去分詞
- □ **switch** 動 切り替える, 切り替わる
- □ **sword** 名 ①剣, 刀 ②武力
- □ **swordsmen** 名 swordsman (剣士, 剣術家) の複数形
- □ **symbol** 名 シンボル, 象徴
- □ **symbolic** 形 象徴する, 象徴的な
- □ **sympathetic** 形 同情する, 思いやりのある
- □ **sympathizer** 名 シンパ, 共鳴者, 支持者
- □ **synergy** 名 相乗効果
- □ **systematically** 副 体系的に, 組織的に, 制度的に

T

- □ **tactician** 名 戦術家
- □ **Takamori** 名 西郷 隆盛《日本の武士 (薩摩藩士)・軍人・政治家, 1828–1877》
- □ **take** 熟 **take a dog for a walk** 犬を散歩させる **take away** ①連れ去る ②取り上げる, 奪い去る ③取り除く **take care of** 〜の世話をする, 〜面倒を見る, 〜を管理する **take down** 下げる, 降ろす **take good care of** 〜を大事に扱う, 大切にする **take 〜 hard** 〜が(精神的に)こたえる **take on** 雇う, (仕事などを)引き受ける, 迎え入れる **take place** 行われる, 起こる **take someone through** (人)に(場所)を通らせる **take up** 取り上げる, 拾い上げる **take up residence in** 〜に居を構える
- □ **talent** 名 才能, 才能ある人
- □ **talented** 形 才能のある, 有能な
- □ **tame** 動 飼いならす, 従わせる
- □ **tangled** 形 込み入った, 複雑に絡

113

SAIGŌ TAKAMORI

み合った

- □ **target** 名 標的, 目的物, 対象 動 的
  [目標]にする
- □ **task** 名 (やるべき)仕事, 職務, 課題
  not up to the task 役割を果たせな
  い
- □ **Tatsumi Naofumi** 立見 尚文
  《桑名藩士, 日本の裁判官・陸軍軍人。
  陸軍大将, 男爵, 1845–1907》
- □ **tax** 名 税
- □ **taxation** 名 課税, 徴税
- □ **technologically** 副 技術的に
- □ **technology** 名 テクノロジー, 科
  学技術
- □ **tell of** ～について話す[説明する]
- □ **temporal** 形 現世の
- □ **Tenshō-In** 名 天璋院《篤子が家定
  の死後に, 落飾して称した戒名》
- □ **Terada-ya inn** 寺田屋《京都伏見
  の船宿》
- □ **terrain** 名 地形, 地勢
- □ **territory** 名 ①領土 ②(広い)地域,
  範囲, 領域
- □ **thanks to** ～のおかげで, ～の結
  果
- □ **that** 熟 **at that time** その時 **so
  that** ～するために, それで, ～できる
  ように **so ～ that ～** 非常に～なの
  で…
- □ **then** 熟 **by then** その時までに
- □ **Theodore Roosevelt** セオド
  ア・ルーズベルト《アメリカ合衆国の
  軍人, 政治家, 第26代大統領》
- □ **thereafter** 副 それ以来, 従って
- □ **therefore** 副 したがって, それゆ
  え, その結果
- □ **thick** 形 厚い
- □ **think of** ～のことを考える, ～を
  思いつく, 考え出す
- □ **This is it.** もはやこれまで。
- □ **those** 熟 **in those days** あのころ
  は, 当時は **those who ～** する人々

- □ **though** 接 ①～にもかかわら
  ず, ～だが ②たとえ～でも **even
  though ～** であるけれども, ～にもか
  かわらず
- □ **threat** 名 おどし, 脅迫
- □ **threaten** 動 脅かす, おびやかす,
  脅迫する
- □ **thrilled** 形 ぞくぞく, わくわくして
- □ **throne** 名 王座, 王権
- □ **through** 熟 **go through** (困難・
  試練などを)体験[経験]する **take
  someone through** (人)に(場所)を
  通らせる
- □ **throughout** 前 ①～中, ～を通じ
  て ②～のいたるところに
- □ **thus** 副 ①このように ②これだけ
  ③かくて, だから
- □ **time** 熟 **at that time** その時 **in no
  time** すぐに, 一瞬で **not have any
  time to ～** する暇がまったくない
- □ **tiny** 形 ちっぽけな, とても小さい
- □ **tip** 名 先端, 頂点
- □ **tired** 形 ①疲れた, くたびれた ②
  あきた, うんざりした
- □ **tired of** 《be ～》～に飽きて[うん
  ざりして]いる
- □ **toady** 名 ゴマすり, 太鼓持ち
- □ **Toba** 名 鳥羽《京都南郊の地名》
- □ **Toba-Fushimi** 《the battle of ～》
  鳥羽・伏見の戦い《戊辰戦争の緒戦と
  なった戦い, 明治元年 / 慶応4年1月3
  日–6日(1868年1月27日–30日)》
- □ **Tokugawa Iemochi** 徳川 家茂
  《江戸幕府第14代征夷大将軍, 在職:
  1858–1866》
- □ **Tokugawa Iesada** 徳川 家定
  《江戸幕府第13代征夷大将軍, 在職:
  1853–1858》
- □ **Tokugawa Yoshinobu** 徳川
  慶喜《江戸幕府第15代征夷大将軍, 在
  職: 1866–1867》
- □ **Tokyo** 名 東京《地名》
- □ **toll** 名 通行料金, 使用料

114

WORD LIST

- [ ] **too** 熟 **far too** あまりにも～過ぎる
- [ ] **torn apart** 引き裂かれる
- [ ] **torture** 動 拷問にかける，ひどく苦しめる
- [ ] **Tosa** 名 土佐藩
- [ ] **totally** 副 全体的に，すっかり
- [ ] **tough** 形 堅い，丈夫な，たくましい，骨の折れる，困難な
- [ ] **track** 名 通った跡 **keep track of** ～の経過を追う，～の記録をつける
- [ ] **trade** 名 取引，貿易，商業 動 取引する，貿易する，商売する
- [ ] **trading** 名 貿易，通商
- [ ] **tradition** 名 伝統，伝説，しきたり
- [ ] **traditional** 形 伝統的な
- [ ] **tragic** 形 悲劇の，痛ましい
- [ ] **training** 名 トレーニング，訓練
- [ ] **traitor** 名 反逆者，裏切り者
- [ ] **transfer** 名 ①移動，移送 ②譲渡
- [ ] **transformation** 名 変化，変換，変容
- [ ] **transition** 名 移り変わり，移行，変遷
- [ ] **treason** 名 裏切り［反逆］行為，背信
- [ ] **treat** 動 扱う
- [ ] **treatment** 名 取り扱い，待遇
- [ ] **treaty** 名 条約，協定
- [ ] **troop** 名 隊
- [ ] **truly** 副 ①全く，本当に，真に ②心から，誠実に
- [ ] **trust** 動 信用［信頼］する 名 信用，信頼
- [ ] **Tsugumichi** 名 西郷 従道《日本の武士（薩摩藩士），陸軍および海軍軍人，政治家。西郷隆盛の弟。1843–1902》
- [ ] **turbulence** 名 大荒れ，騒乱，乱気流
- [ ] **turmoil** 名 動揺，騒動，混乱
- [ ] **turn down** 拒絶する
- [ ] **turn into** ～に変わる

- [ ] **turn to** ～の方を向く，～に頼る，～に変わる
- [ ] **typical** 形 典型的な，象徴的な

U

- [ ] **unbelievably** 副 信じられないほど
- [ ] **uncomfortable** 形 心地よくない
- [ ] **underdeveloped** 形 発展［発達］の遅れた
- [ ] **underestimate** 動 安く見積もる，過小評価する，見くびる
- [ ] **understanding** 名 理解，意見の一致，了解
- [ ] **unemployed** 名 《the –》失業者
- [ ] **unfair** 形 不公平な，不当な
- [ ] **unfairly** 副 不当に
- [ ] **unfortunate** 形 不運な，あいにくな，不適切な
- [ ] **unfortunately** 副 不幸にも，運悪く
- [ ] **unhappy** 形 不運な，不幸な
- [ ] **unify** 動 一つにする，統一する
- [ ] **unite** 動 ①1つにする［なる］，合わせる，結ぶ ②結束する，団結する
- [ ] **united** 形 団結した，まとまった，連合した
- [ ] **unsupportive** 形 支えとならない，支持しない
- [ ] **unveiling** 名 ベールをとること，除幕（式）**unveiling ceremony** 除幕式
- [ ] **up to** ～まで，～に至るまで，～に匹敵して
- [ ] **upheaval** 名 大変動，激変
- [ ] **upon** 前 ①《場所・接触》～（の上）に ②《日・時》～に ③《関係・従事》～に関して，～について，～して **be infringed upon** 侵害される
- [ ] **upset** 動 気を悪くさせる，（心・神

115

SAIGŌ TAKAMORI

経など)をかき乱す
- □ **urge** 動《 – … to ～》…に～するよう熱心に勧める
- □ **urging** 名 しつこい懇願と嘆願
- □ **used to** 形《be – 》～に慣れている
- □ **utterly** 副 まったく, 完全に

V

- □ **value** 名 価値, 値打ち, 価格 **of value** 貴重な, 価値のある
- □ **vessel** 名(大型の)船
- □ **victory** 名 勝利, 優勝
- □ **view** 熟 **point of view** 考え方, 視点
- □ **violent** 形 暴力的な, 激しい
- □ **visible** 形 目に見える, 明らかな
- □ **vital** 形 きわめて重要な
- □ **vividly** 副 生き生きと, 鮮やかに
- □ **volcano** 名 火山 **active volcano** 活火山
- □ **vulnerable** 形 傷つきやすい, もろい

W

- □ **wage** 動(戦争・闘争などを)行う
- □ **walk** 熟 **take a dog for a walk** 犬を散歩させる
- □ **war** 熟 **civil war** 内戦, 内乱
- □ **warehouse** 名 倉庫
- □ **warfare** 名 戦争, 交戦状態, 戦闘行為
- □ **warn** 動 警告する, 用心させる
- □ **warrior** 名 戦士, 軍人
- □ **warrior-class** 名 武士階級
- □ **wave** 名 波
- □ **waver** 動 心が揺らぐ, 揺れ動く, ぐらつく

- □ **way** 熟 **along the way** 途中で **by the way** ところで **on one's way to** ～に行く途中で **way to** ～する方法
- □ **weaken** 動 弱くなる, 弱める
- □ **weapon** 名 武器, 兵器
- □ **weigh** 動(重さを)はかる
- □ **well** 熟 **as well as** ～と同様に
- □ **western** 形 ①西の, 西側の ②《W-》西洋の 名《W-》西部劇, ウェスタン
- □ **Westerner** 名 欧米人, 西洋人
- □ **whatever** 代 ①《関係代名詞》～するものは何でも ②どんなこと[もの]が～とも 形 ①どんな～でも ②《否定文・疑問文で》少しの～も, 何らかの
- □ **whenever** 接 ①～するときはいつでも, ～するたびに ②いつ～しても
- □ **whether** 接 ～かどうか, ～かまたは…, ～であろうとなかろうと **whether or not** ～かどうか
- □ **whisper** 動 ささやく, 小声で話す
- □ **who** 熟 **those who** ～する人々
- □ **whom** 代 ①誰を[に] ②《関係代名詞》～するところの人, そしてその人を
- □ **widely** 副 広く, 広範囲にわたって
- □ **widow** 名 未亡人
- □ **win someone over** ～に認めてもらう, 味方に引き入れる
- □ **winner** 名 勝利者, 成功者
- □ **withdrew** 動 withdraw(引っ込める)の過去
- □ **within** 前 ①～の中[内]に, ～の内部に ②～以内で, ～を越えないで
- □ **withstand** 動 抵抗する, 逆らう
- □ **wonder** 動 ①不思議に思う, (～に)驚く ②(～かしらと)思う **wonder about** ～を怪しむ **wonder if** ～ではないかと思う
- □ **word** 熟 **in other words** すなわち, 言い換えれば

116

WORD LIST

- **work against** ～に反する働きをする，～に反対する
- **worn out** 擦り切れた
- **worse** 副 いっそう悪く
- **wound** 名 傷
- **wrangling** 名 口論，論争
- **wrestling** 名 レスリング sumo wrestling 相撲

Y

- **Yamaoka Tesshū** 山岡 鉄舟《幕末から明治時代の幕臣，政治家，思想家，1836–1888》
- **yet** 熟 not yet まだ～してない
- **Yoshinobu** 名 徳川 慶喜《江戸幕府第15代征夷大将軍，在職：1866–1867》
- **youth** 名 若さ，元気，若者

English Conversational Ability Test
国際英語会話能力検定

● **E-CATとは…**
英語が話せるようになるための
テストです。インターネット
ベースで、30分であなたの発
話力をチェックします。

www.ecatexam.com

● **iTEP®とは…**
世界各国の企業、政府機関、アメリカの大学
300校以上が、英語能力判定テストとして採用。
オンラインによる90分のテストで文法、リー
ディング、リスニング、ライティング、スピー
キングの5技能をスコア化。iTEP®は、留学、就
職、海外赴任などに必要な、世界に通用する英
語力を総合的に評価する画期的なテストです。

www.itepexamjapan.com

ラダーシリーズ
Saigō Takamori 西郷隆盛

2018年1月5日　第1刷発行

著　者　西海コエン

発行者　浦　晋亮

発行所　IBCパブリッシング株式会社
〒162-0804 東京都新宿区中里町29番3号
菱秀神楽坂ビル9F
Tel. 03-3513-4511　Fax. 03-3513-4512
www.ibcpub.co.jp

© Coen Nishiumi 2018
© IBC Publishing, Inc. 2018

印刷　株式会社シナノパブリッシングプレス
装丁　伊藤理恵
組版データ　Adobe Caslon Pro Regular + Footlight MT Light Regular

落丁本・乱丁本は、小社宛にお送りください。送料小社負担にてお取り替えいたします。本書の無断複写(コピー)は著作権法上での例外を除き禁じられています。

Printed in Japan
ISBN978-4-7946-0520-7